Stephen Davey

WISDOM COMMENTARY SERIES

RUTH

CHARITY HOUSE
PUBLISHERS

Wisdom Commentary Series: Ruth

Author: Stephen Davey
Editor: Lalanne Barber
Cover Design and Body Layout: Grace Gourley
Photo of Stephen: Sam Gray Portraits, Raleigh, NC (samgrayportraits.com)
ISBN 978 0 9851679 1 2

Unless otherwise noted, all Scripture quotations are from the New American Standard Bible®,
© 1960, 1962, 1963, 1968, 1971, 1972, 1973, 1975, 1995 by the Lockman Foundation. Used by
permission.

Published by Charity House Publishers

Charity House Publishers, Inc.
2201 Candun Street
Suite 103
Apex, NC 27523-6412
USA
www.wisdomonline.org

To Candace & Charity,
my daughers, my joy;
who await the coming of their princes—
young men who will be completely unworthy,
yet entirely blessed by the gifts
of their never-ending love.

CONTENTS

CHAPTER ONE

ONCE UPON A TIME . . .

An Introduction

H ere's a poem that makes men cringe with embarrassment and women sigh in exasperation:

> *Roses are red,*
> *Violets are blue,*
> *Daffodils cost thirty bucks,*
> *Will dandelions do?*

Perhaps that's why so many women can identify with a single gal who had been dating a guy for several years and had tried everything to get him to make a commitment. Nothing worked and she had pretty much given up. She placed an ad in the classifieds that simply read "Husband Wanted" and listed her phone number.

The next day she received more than a hundred phone calls from women and they all said the same thing: "You can have mine."

Ah, the damage of dandelions.

So what are kids picking up from older people about romance and love? Two kids responded to the question, "How does true love happen?"

Nine-year-old philosopher Roger gave his opinion on love when he said, "Falling in love is like an avalanche . . . you gotta run for your life!"

From the feminine perspective, nine-year-old Janet replied, "No one is sure how love happens, but I heard it has something to do with how you smell."

I'll never forget when my younger daughter was around eleven years old, and we were riding somewhere in my pickup truck. I asked her if she'd ever been kissed?

She said, "No, sir." She was dead serious.

I said, "Honey, that's just great."

Then she added, "But after Sunday school a couple of weeks ago, a boy tried to kiss me."

I said, "He did?" My initial thought was church discipline. Instead, I asked her, "Well, what did you *do*?"

She said, "I punched him in the stomach."

"Right there in the classroom?"

"Yes, sir."

I said, "That's terrific, honey . . . way to go!"

That'll redefine the right hand of fellowship. Not to worry—romance eventually catches up with age . . . it's the stuff of girls' dreams early on. Eventually they stop swinging.

Unless you've consigned the book of fairytales to a cluttered shelf in the garage—next to your bouquet of wilted dandelions—as a dad, you've probably spent some time reading a few tales of romance and rescue to your daughter.

Both of my girls sat on my lap as I read to them from the classics. They loved hearing the enchanted stories of Cinderella, Snow White, and Sleeping Beauty. Although they heard the same stories over and over again, their anticipation and excitement grew whenever it was time for Prince Charming to finally show up.

We enjoy a good fairytale, but we also know they really don't come true. They're just make-believe . . . they never pan out.

One did.

It has all the elements of an instant classic: a depressed widowed mother-in-law; a beautiful but poor damsel in distress; a wealthy prince who rides by on his horse and saves the day.

J. Vernon McGee wrote, "The Book of Ruth reads like a novel, but it is *not* fiction."[1]

That's right—this one took place long, long ago . . . once upon a time.

There isn't any evidence of wicked witches, poison apples, or glass slippers. But *this* one's for real. God recorded the story. And there's plenty of evidence that God's hand is at work behind the scenes, arranging all the details so that the damsel in distress will be rescued at just the right time, in just the right way, and by just the right man.

God didn't just record the story . . . He *wrote* it. And according to centuries of Jewish tradition, God used His prophet Samuel to provide all the details for future generations to read.[2]

The opening lines prepare us for a tale of romance and rescue. The first few words ***Now it came about in the days when . . .*** (Ruth 1:1) sound a lot like "Once upon a time . . ."

Before we turn the first page in this classic love story, let's examine several reasons why God preserved this for us through the pen of Samuel.

DEMONSTRATION OF THE GOSPEL OF GRACE

You might miss the richness of this truth if you read the story too quickly. In the Hebrew culture, Ruth was one of five scrolls that would be read annually at a Jewish festival. Other scrolls read were Esther at the Feast of Purim, Ecclesiastes at the Feast of Tabernacles, and Ruth at the Feast of Weeks, also known as Pentecost.[3]

It isn't a coincidence that the love story of a kinsman redeemer winning his bride would be read at the Feast of Pentecost where, centuries later, *the* Kinsman Redeemer initiated the redeeming of His Bride as the Church was created.

The perfect timing of divine love and grace become the backdrop in this tale of romance and redemption. We will be introduced to a Gentile girl who is a descendant of Moab, condemned by God's law and even forbidden worship in God's temple: *"No Ammonite or Moabite shall enter the assembly of the LORD"* (Deuteronomy 23:3).

Boaz will eventually redeem her (paralleling our own redemption), not because she met the requirements of the Law but because of his grace and love for her.

The Law declared, "Keep out!" Grace exclaimed, "Welcome home!"

ILLUSTRATION OF THE LOVE OF CHRIST

The Book of Ruth provides the only detailed example in the Bible of the Hebrew *goel*—kinsman redeemer. The Law of Moses allowed for a near relative or kinsman to marry the widow of the deceased in order to provide everything she needed, including an heir to the deceased's estate.

Not just anyone could marry the widow. He had to be a relative of the family. And the closest family member had the right of first refusal, as we'll discover later.

Boaz was related to Naomi's husband and could legally redeem Ruth if he chose to do so. By this redemptive purchase, he would become an illustration of Jesus redeeming His beloved Bride.

In this tale of romance, we discover an often overlooked requirement met by virtue of the incarnation of God the Son. He became a human being—our *relative*—in order to qualify as our *goel* . . . our Kinsman redeemer.

Paul emphasized this point as he wrote to the Galatians,

> *But when the fullness of the time came, God sent forth His Son, born of a woman, born under the Law, so that He might redeem those who were under the Law* (Galatians 4:4–5).

Keep in mind, according to the Law of Moses, Boaz cannot be forced to take upon himself the responsibilities of Ruth's bankrupt estate. Frankly, it isn't his problem . . . unless he wants it to be.

Likewise, Jesus Christ was not responsible for the sinful bankruptcy of the human race, yet He accepted that responsibility when *He Himself bore our sins in His body on the cross, so that we might die to sin and live to righteousness* (1 Peter 2:24).

Consider, also, the fact that Boaz could have chosen to select a more eligible bride, untainted with idolatry and uncondemned by the Law of Moses. But he illustrates Christ, who chose to redeem a soiled and sinful Bride, loving us *while we were yet sinners* (Romans 5:8).

And just as Boaz had to be wealthy enough to buy the estate of Elimelech, *we have redemption through His blood, the forgiveness of our trespasses, according to the riches of His grace, which He lavished on us* (Ephesians 1:7–8).

Boaz will redeem his bride with his own money. Jesus will redeem His Bride with *His own precious blood* (1 Peter 1:19). Our redemption was no less an act of gracious affection and love than the redemption of Ruth. Both transactions were neither cold nor emotionless.

Jesus Christ isn't saying, "Okay, I'll take Stephen and Frank and Marsha and Susan and, well, alright, I'll guess you'll do, too."

Not at all.

The redemption of one sinner is cause for celebration and joy among the hosts of heaven throughout the farthest reaches of God's glory *(Luke 15:10)*.

When did the awakening of redeemed sinners and the calling of sinners to join the bridal party become a cold emotionless transaction by our Savior? Perhaps our own Church history has separated the romance and delight from the heart and passion of God's bride-winning Son.

Puritans and early American theologians, e.g., Jonathan Edwards in *The History of Redemption* and Stuart Robinson's work on *The Discourse of Redemption*, omitted any reference to the Book of Ruth as they traced the history of redemption through the Old Testament. They understood the concepts of redemption, but they often missed the romance of redemption.

J. Vernon McGee wrote, "Earlier treatments created a view that redemption was a rather cold transaction . . . a thousand times no! Redemption is the love story of a Kinsman who neither counted the cost nor figured up the profit and loss, but for joy paid an exorbitant price for one that He loved."[4]

He went on to make this comment: "The Book of Ruth declares that redemption is not a business transaction . . . it is a love [story]."[5]

The Book of Ruth not only demonstrates the work of grace and the love of Christ—there's more.

DESIGNATION OF THE LINEAGE OF JESUS CHRIST

The clear line between David and Judah—the tribal line of the coming King—is provided in Ruth. In fact, the last Old Testament genealogy showing the descent of Jesus from King David is the genealogical table found at the end of Ruth.

Ruth's genealogy will be borrowed and repeated by both Matthew and Luke in their genealogy of Jesus Christ.

So critical is the link that Ruth provides, Old Testament scholars Keil and Delitzsch believe it is the *primary* reason the Book of Ruth was recorded.[6] And for good reason. It is the singular record in Ruth which provides Matthew and Luke with enough information to prove that Jesus Christ is indeed a descendant of the royal line of David.

Also discovered in the genealogical record of Ruth is the wonderful fact that Boaz's Gentile mother didn't marry just any Jewish man—she married a man from the royal line of Judah *(Matthew 1:5–6)*, which makes Jesus not only the legal heir to the throne of David but also to the role of Israel's High Priest, making His bride eligible to reign with Him.

He is truly our King, High Priest, and Redeemer.

ASPIRATION OF GODLY LIVING

This fairytale begins with the word ***And*** or ***Now***, depending on the translation you use. Ruth is a companion volume to the Book of Judges.

> ***Now it came about in the days when the judges governed . . .***
> (Ruth 1:1).

What was it like to live during the days of the judges? All you have to do is look across from the first page of Ruth to the last page of Judges to read the answer:

> *In those days there was no king in Israel; and everyone did what was right in his own eyes* (Judges 21:25).

This immediately informs us that the beautiful love story of Boaz and Ruth will shine against the dark, troubled, sinful, anything-goes immoral backdrop of their present generation.

One author wrote that the Book of Ruth is a pearl in the pig pen of the judges.[7] These are the dark days of the judges, when everyone did that which was right in their own eyes.

You might be tempted to read the Book of Ruth and assume it was a great time to be a follower of God—that all men were kind and godly toward women, and women were discreet and respectful toward men. You might get the impression that all landowners cared about their employees, and business owners were generous with their profits, helping those in need.

Hardly—which makes the love story of Boaz and Ruth all the more remarkable.

What were the days of the judges like? These days were the lowest points in the history of Israel—days of division, cruelty, apostasy, civil war, and national disgrace.[8]

Many Old Testament scholars believe Boaz was a contemporary of Gideon. Some like to believe that Boaz served for a time under the command of this former judge—that they even knew each other.

We can't be sure, but we do know that Gideon's biography goes from good to ungodly. He eventually marries a number of women who bear 70 sons, and as soon as Gideon dies, one son has all the others killed, only to be assassinated later by the very people he ruled *(Judges 9)*.

It's quite possible that Boaz lived during the days of another well-known judge named Samson. Samson's biography was hardly any better. He moved from one bedroom to another until he told his secret to his final mistress. Delilah cut off his hair one night and the Philistines captured this wayward judge, putting out his eyes and trampling the integrity of God and all who followed Him *(Judges 16)*.

There was also that horrible event of the Levite who took a mistress from the town of Boaz to Ephraim, where she was tragically gang raped and killed. The story spread throughout the entire Jewish world. It would have been front page news in the *Bethlehem Times*.

So much for the days of the judges.

Boaz and Ruth didn't have many models. They lived during difficult days when godly decisions were minority opinion.

Frankly, there is *never* an easy time to do the right thing.

Finding a spouse, raising a family, developing a business or ministry, anything that glorifies God is always a minority position in life—perhaps even in the Church. And yet, in the lives of Boaz and Ruth, you have the encouraging witness of:

- the sanctuary of a godly home;

- the commitment to humble service to those in need;

- the description of godly manhood that shepherds a family;
- the presentation of godly womanhood that pursues a virtuous life;
- the sanctity of the marriage vow;
- the fidelity of marriage when mistresses were as common as wives.

These were the dark days of the judges . . . and this is the shining testimony of Boaz and Ruth who witnessed to the possibility of:

- living a godly life in the midst of an ungodly culture;
- staying pure when surrounded by impurity;
- not allowing culture to rewrite their character;
- allowing, instead, their character to influence a generation and those beyond.

The Book of Ruth demonstrates the grace of God, the love of Christ, the proof of Christ's lineage, and the witness that godliness is possible even in ungodly times.

REVELATION OF GOD'S PROVIDENCE IN THE SMALLEST DETAILS

Here's a quick overview of some of the *coincidental* details:

- The patriarch of this family Elimelech, in disobedience, just happens to move to Moab;
- One of his sons, in his own rebellion, just happens to marry Ruth;
- Ruth just happens to desire to follow after God and return to Israel with Naomi ten years later;
- Ruth just happens to glean in a field which just happened to belong to one of Naomi's relatives;
- And he just happened to be riding his horse out to the field on the very day when Ruth just happened to choose his field in which to forage for grain;
- And he just happened to be a godly single man, the son of a Gentile woman who had also converted to Judaism years earlier;
- And so it just happened that Boaz and Ruth got married and carried on the line of the Messiah—a lineage that now mixed Jewish and

Gentile blood, ultimately bearing a Messiah who would win a Bride among both Jewish and Gentile believers.

Isn't it amazing how that all just *happened?*

Not quite. This Book will reveal that God is the Director in the symphony of life and He orchestrates everything to fulfill His purposes. Some events make sense to us now and some of them will not make sense for generations to come.

At the outset of this dramatic tale:

- Boaz could be thinking, *Why doesn't God give me a wife?*

- Naomi is asking, "Why did God take away my husband?"

- Ruth will be wondering, *What kind of God have I decided to follow?*

- And even Elimelech must have thought sometime before he died, *My faithlessness to God has ruined everything . . . it's all lost.*

They have no idea . . . truth is, we don't either. So as we pick up our storybook and the storyline begins to unfold, take heart, my friend—God just so happens to be the One writing your story, too.

The best thing to do is follow His lead . . . submit to each stroke of His quill as He crafts a tale that, in the end, will fit His purpose and be for His glory, giving you the greatest satisfaction—and certainly the greatest ending of any story: a future glory with Him.

Our lives simply become the parchment upon which our sovereign Lord writes His purposes and His plans . . . His storyline for us . . . His drama.

No failure is final; no fear is fatal. You are *His* story.

Be like the college student who stood up in front of her peers at the end of a mission conference, held up a sheet of paper, and said, "This blank piece of paper represents my life, now dedicated to Christ. It symbolizes that I am open to whatever He wants to write into my life . . . I'm willing for anything." Then she added, "The only thing I've done at the bottom of the page is sign my name—everything is yet unknown, but I've already signed on . . . my life is His."

Sounds a lot like Boaz and Ruth.

And so this fairytale begins: "Once upon a time . . ."

Now it came about in the days when the judges governed, that there was a famine in the land. And a certain man of Bethlehem in Judah went to sojourn in the land of Moab with his wife and his two sons. ²The name of the man was Elimelech, and the name of his wife, Naomi; and the names of his two sons were Mahlon and Chilion, Ephrathites of Bethlehem in Judah. Now they entered the land of Moab and remained there. ³Then Elimelech, Naomi's husband, died; and she was left with her two sons. ⁴They took for themselves Moabite women as wives; the name of the one was Orpah and the name of the other Ruth. And they lived there about ten years. ⁵Then both Mahlon and Chilion also died, and the woman was bereft of her two children and her husband.

–Ruth 1:1–5

CHAPTER TWO

GREENER GRASS

Ruth 1:1–5

As I drive to and from my home, there is a pasture on the side of the road where several horses graze. In spite of the fact that their pasture is fertile and green, it's not unusual to see one of them straining over the top rail of the fence to try to get a mouthful of grass on the other side near the road.

The curious thing to me is that the grass is not nearly as plentiful or luxuriant. It never fails to remind me of the myth of *greener grass*—the noodling thought that, somewhere, life is better . . . easier . . . happier.

It certainly can't be in the middle of *our* own pasture.

Life would be better at a different job with a higher paycheck—living in a bigger house, in a more affluent neighborhood, with a newer model car in the driveway. Life would be easier at another school, with a more interesting faculty and a nicer roommate. Life would be more fulfilling with better health, a more attentive spouse, well-behaved children, and a wider circle of friends.

Truly, the grass is always greener everywhere else but *here*.

We can't ignore the fact that some situations are harder than others. And sometimes we need to make the right changes for the right reasons. But when problems crop up, we are too quick to conclude that surely God would not *purposefully* make life difficult, uncomfortable, or challenging.

Most assuredly, He wants everyone to be happy. Isn't greener grass the evidence of God's leading?

Erma Bombeck had a funny way of summing up the myth when she entitled her book *The Grass Is Always Greener over the Septic Tank*. The truth is greener grass might be the most dangerous pit you'll ever avoid. It looks so promising—so rewarding—but you have no idea what's underneath.

We are about to witness this dangerous myth play out in living color in the lives of real people. If you've ever read a fairytale to your child, the story becomes dark and troubled after a page or two. Storm clouds gather on the horizon.

In the fairytale of Boaz and Ruth, which, by the way, happens to be real, a similar storyline emerges. After only a few lines, the clouds begin to roll in.

THE CRISIS

Samuel records:

> **Now it came about in the days when the judges governed,**
> **that there was a famine in the land. And a certain man of**
> **Bethlehem in Judah went to sojourn in the land of Moab**
> **with his wife and his two sons** (Ruth 1:1).

Without a doubt, this man, his wife, and two sons are facing a genuine crisis. And that's when thoughts of greener grass are usually sown in the soil of our hearts.

For this family, a famine in the land impacted their hometown of Bethlehem. Add to their crisis the political upheaval during the days of the judges: the collapse of civility, morality, and true religious piety.

Compound the crisis with living in fear of a Midianite attack, resulting in the loss of cattle . . . or your life. Then mix in the fact that any investment potential in the land of Bethlehem never would have looked more unpromising.

Factor in one more ingredient: the cupboard is empty and so is the hayloft. This man decides that greener grass can be found anywhere but here.

And the irony or pun in the Hebrew language would have been immediately recognized by Jewish readers: *Famine in the land—and a man from Bethlehem.* Bethlehem meant *house of bread.* In other words, the bread basket of Judah is empty. People who live in the *house of bread* are going *hungry.*[1]

The original audience would have immediately caught this contradiction in terms: "There is a famine in the house of bread." That's like saying there is an increase in gang warfare in Philadelphia, the City of Brotherly Love or a rise in demonic activity in Los Angeles, the City of Angels.[2]

The association of famine with Bethlehem—the bread basket of Judah—would have created an obvious twist in this story. Bethlehem lay about six miles south of Jerusalem and its name House of Bread was evidently well earned. Wheat, barley, olives, almonds, and grapes were plentiful in ancient times.[3]

Not anymore.

More than likely, this is the famine mentioned in *Judges 6*, which helps us place this story within the leadership of Gideon and the oppression of the Midianites. Even more importantly, it helps us understand that this famine was a result of the Israelites' rebellion against God.

God often used physical famine to bring the nation to their sense of spiritual need. And God's plan would not have included people leaving the House of Bread for greener pastures but to repent and obey His Word.

To this day, God uses days of need—of famine, if you will—to refashion faith in His path, His promises, and His provision. This was a crisis that developed character; it was testing that deepened trust.

To add even more to the play on word meanings is the fact that this family will move to Moab. The Lord called Moab a *washbowl (Psalm 60:8)*. A washbowl was used to wash dirty feet. It would be akin to calling Moab a trash can—a plot of ground where you dumped things you wanted to throw away. Moab was a spiritual wasteland.

So here you have a Jewish family, facing a crisis of faith, who choose to abandon the House of Bread and move to the Place of Trash. They effectively moved from the *bread*basket to the *waste*basket.

THE CHARACTERS

There are six key players in this drama so far, and after the opening verses, only three are still alive.

The patriarch of the family was named **Elimelech** *(Ruth 1:2)*. Loosely translated, his name meant *God is my King*.[4] The tragedy of Elimelech's life was simply the fact that he didn't live up to his name.

Listed next is **Naomi** *(gracious one)* his wife, and Naomi and Elimelech's sons, who make a rather brief curtain call. Their names are **Mahlon** and

Chilion. These boys had rhyming names in Hebrew, implying they could have been twins. More than likely, their mother, like many mothers, just wanted her children's names to rhyme.

My ministry-minded parents named their four sons Daniel, Stephen, Timothy, and Jonathan. When my father introduced us at any church where he was preaching, he'd usually say, "We have four sons: two from the Old Testament and two from the New Testament." Certainly sounds spiritually minded, doesn't it? My mother couldn't resist giving the firstborn our father's name as the middle name, and giving the rest of us middle names that all started with D: Duane, Dean, and Dale.

Three D's . . . looked a lot like my report card growing up!

Maybe Naomi had a little paperback book *200 Hebrew Names That Rhyme*. The reason I suggest this, somewhat tongue-in-cheek, yet somewhat seriously, is that Naomi evidently wanted rhyming names more than she wanted names with significant meanings. **Mahlon** means *puny* or *weakling*, and **Chilion** means *complaining* or *pining*.

Imagine naming your two sons Puny and Whiney. Way to go, Mom. Thank you for giving them those handles for the rest of their lives!

While we're at it, we have the names of their future wives in ***Ruth 1:4***: **Orpah** means *obstinate*—literally *strong neck*.[5] What a lovely name for a girl! Finally, there's **Ruth**, whose name means *comfort* or, perhaps, *friend*.[6]

So, here you have Mister Puny marrying Miss Strong Neck, and Mister Whiny marrying Miss Comfort. Frankly, Ruth is the only one who doesn't seem to fit this family portrait.

Remarkably, they all play out the meanings of their names in one way or another. All, that is, except one.

The only character who didn't live up to his name was the one who really should have: **Elimelech** . . . Mister My-God-is-King. In other words, *God is the master* of my life. *God is pre-eminent* in my decision making. God comes first.

Well, not quite, for Elimelech.

I want to point out one more thing about this family: we're told that they were ***Ephrathites of Bethlehem*** (Ruth 1:2). Ephrath was the name of the wife of Caleb, the famous fearless colleague of Joshua. According to *1 Chronicles 2:19*, Caleb's descendants settled Bethlehem.

Ephrathites were members of a clan that held the prominent position of being one of the *first* families . . . they were among the aristocracy of the town of Bethlehem.[7] That simply underscores the riches-to-rags crisis hitting this particular family.

What you have here are the Rockefellers threatened with eviction . . . the Vanderbilts, homeless and hungry.

Why stay in Bethlehem where the famine has reduced them—and everyone else—to handouts? They're used to a better life than this. Why should they stay in the land of their faith and forefathers when the grass is so much greener in Moab?

This crisis will lead these characters to justify compromise.

THE COMPROMISE

From the ridge of hills on the edge of Bethlehem you can see the land of Moab. Moab was well-watered by winter rains that were driven inland by the winds of the Mediterranean Sea.[8]

Elimelech no doubt stood on that ridge in Bethlehem, surrounded by dry grass and parched brown fields. On a clear day he could see the fertile fields of Moab, less than fifty miles away and just on the other side of the Dead Sea.

Maybe he thought to himself, *I'll only go for a short while. God won't mind. Our flight from His land and His people will be over before you know it and we'll be back home facing better days.*

- **verse 1** – [a certain man] ***went to* sojourn** – refers to a temporary stay

- **verse 2** – [they entered] ***the land of Moab . . . and* remained *there*** – a word for settling down

- **verse 4** – ***they lived there about* ten years** – what an astounding discovery!

Notice the progressive terms used. Learn from Elimelech the danger of greener grass: it can turn into a swamp. Greener grass is often quicksand in disguise. But that doesn't mean it immediately felt like quicksand to Elimelech. In fact, their move was evidently successful: ten years of provision, a place to live, and even brides for their sons.

God must not have minded the move after all . . . or did He?

Don't overlook the fact that this family knowingly forfeited participation in the assembly of the Lord. They walked away from a community they should have stayed to help. Elimelech could have led his people to repent and worship the true and living God. Instead, he ran away. He viewed the greener pastures in Moab as worth more than worship and fellowship with the assembly *(Deuteronomy 23:3)*.

No wonder these opening verses form the only part of this entire book where God is not addressed, consulted, or even mentioned.

Elimelech could have argued—and probably did, at first: *I'm not going to become a Moabite. C'mon, I would never offer my children or grandchildren to Chemosh, the god of the Moabites. I'm not into child sacrifice or idolatry; I would never do that or condone that. Hey, I'm not a Moabite—I'm just going to temporarily, you know, forsake God's Word and the worship of God to go live with some Moabites until the storm blows over. I'll come back . . . eventually.*

And before you know it, sometime before his death, he picks out a couple of Moabite women for his sons to marry as they settle down in the spiritual wasteland of Moab.

No alarm bells rang, and the covenant promises of land, seed, and all the words of the prophets would slip out of Elimelech's mind and heart until they no longer mattered. They were in Moab to stay.

Pursuing greener grass has a way of lulling our spirit to sleep.

That which seems like a temporary compromise is no big deal:

- just one quick look;
- just one small bet;
- just one tiny sip;
- just one personal expense on my company account;
- just one little lie;
- just one click of the mouse.

And greener grass grows into a tangled wilderness where one can barely see daylight . . . or find the way back home.

Maybe Elimelech never meant to stay . . . perhaps he really did plan to return. But either way, this patriarch of a leading family in Bethlehem scandalized his community and betrayed his faith by moving to Moab.

And he would never come home again.

THE CONSEQUENCES

Greener grass can lead to a graveyard. You can't help but notice how suddenly the writer reports the deaths of these three men:

> ***Then Elimelech, Naomi's husband, died; and she was left with her two sons. . . . Then both Mahlon and Chilion also died*** (Ruth 1:3; 5).

There's no explanation. No coroner's report. Just headline news in Bethlehem that Elimelech and his sons are dead.

Many Jewish scholars and Old Testament commentators read between the lines and conclude that the deaths of Naomi's husband and sons were divine judgments upon their actions of unbelief.[9] This is similar to the subtle reference to New Testament believers who had died early deaths because they approached the Lord's table while cherishing, planning, and/or engaging in secret sins *(I Corinthians 11:30).*

Don't miss the fact that the sons of Elimelech disobeyed God by not returning with their father's body for burial. They hadn't even converted their wives to the God of Abraham. They had equal disregard for the Word of God and the will of God. Their early deaths were judgments for having been assimilated into the lifestyle and culture of Moab.

The opening paragraph ends with Naomi virtually alone, ***bereft of her two children and her husband*** (Ruth 1:5).

She must be wondering, *What do I do now? Where did those ten years go?*

Let me offer four observations from this opening scene in our study where we've watched a man move to what he thought was greener grass.

1. One sinful decision is often followed by additional wrong decisions, leading farther away from the path of wisdom.

Maybe you're thinking, *So, what do I do about my sinful decisions? I've made several of them and now I'm off the path and out fellowship with Christ. Do I stay here and die in some spiritually deserted plain like Moab?*

No. Jesus Christ is ever ready to forgive our sin. He's on the lookout for returning renegades . . . people who confess, rather than negotiate . . . runaways who want their relationship restored with Him again.

Jesus specializes in redeeming those runaways and renegades. I'm an eyewitness—and a recipient—of this kind of redeeming grace.

If you are a believer in Christ and you've made sinful decisions that dishonor God, don't let the distance you find yourself from the path of wisdom keep you from taking the first step of genuine repentance.

Just remember, true repentance leads us to take responsibility for the consequences of sin. Repentance doesn't hand it off for someone else to repair the damage; it doesn't sweep the dirt under the carpet—it throws it out.

Renegades who truly return to the House of Bread own up to their sin and accept the consequences that may last longer than they'd like. They become reminders of how dangerous sin can be. They also become daily testimonies of God's grace and forgiveness, as well as revealing His strength in their life as they commit to walking with Him and doing the right thing.

2. Greener grass may seem to make sense, but trusting the Spirit is a different thing altogether.

Greener grass might make wonderful economic sense, yet bring about spiritual loss. It might offer personal advancement but, at the same time, result in spiritual regression.

Let's put this out on the table where we can see it clearly: the real reason greener grass can make so much sense is because our hearts are selfish and corrupt, and our minds are in desperate need of daily renewal and transformation *(Romans 12:1–2)*.

The heart of all our problems is the problem within all our hearts: *we* are our greatest danger to wise living. Because of our sinful hearts, disobedience can actually make sense.

3. Pursuing greener grass rather than the glory of God is the fountainhead of grief.

Imagine, in only five verses you have a huge volume of sorrow and grief. And it all began with a *look* . . . then a *longing* . . . then a *leaving* behind of all once held dear.

A newcomer to our church shared with me the tragic story of his renegade wife. She was an unlikely candidate for choosing a rebel lifestyle: a homeschooling mother of nine children and a committed wife of more than twenty-five years. One day she announced to her husband that she was leaving the family and her marriage for another man she'd met online. To the shock of both husband and children (her youngest was six and her oldest was twenty-four), she turned her back on her family and completely walked away. She left her husband with these words, "I've given you and this family twenty-five years of my life; now it's time for *me*."

The trouble is she left everything behind except a guilty conscience. That would never leave her alone. And she didn't make it too long with her wealthy new friend; she eventually married another. She started drinking along the way and stayed "medicated" all day long to try to numb the searing pain of guilt. Eight short years after leaving her family, she died of liver disease. Her stay in Moab was not quite as long as runaway Elimelech and his two rebel sons.

When you leave the path of obedience, you invite pain to become your traveling companion. Greener grass often disguises greater grief.

4. Famine in the will of God is better than feasting outside the will of God.

Take it from Naomi . . . she learned this the hard way. A short trip became a ten-year stay. Three funerals and three fresh graves brought her to her senses. Perhaps for the first time in a long time she realized how far she was from home.

And this isn't the end of her story—it's merely the prelude to a new beginning she would not even be able to imagine.

Fortunately for all of us, God has a way of finding people who are lost in the middle of Moab—the Trash Dump—and setting their feet back on the path to Bethlehem, the House of Bread.

He never forces our feet to move. The path back will always begin with fresh surrender and repentant trust. But the good news of grace is that God has a way of redeeming wasted years and foolish decisions.

Like the prodigal's father in Luke's Gospel, God is waiting to offer fellowship to runaways who return to that place where they left the path—the place where they will begin to write a new chapter in their relationship with Jesus Christ . . . a most gracious, forgiving Kinsman Redeemer.

⁶Then she arose with her daughters-in-law that she might return from the land of Moab, for she had heard in the land of Moab that the LORD had visited His people in giving them food. ⁷So she departed from the place where she was, and her two daughters-in-law with her; and they went on the way to return to the land of Judah. ⁸And Naomi said to her two daughters-in-law, "Go, return each of you to her mother's house. May the LORD deal kindly with you as you have dealt with the dead and with me. ⁹May the LORD grant that you may find rest, each in the house of her husband." Then she kissed them, and they lifted up their voices and wept. ¹⁰And they said to her, "No, but we will surely return with you to your people." ¹¹But Naomi said, "Return, my daughters. Why should you go with me? Have I yet sons in my womb, that they may be your husbands? ¹²Return, my daughters! Go, for I am too old to have a husband. If I said I have hope, if I should even have a husband tonight and also bear sons, ¹³would you therefore wait until they were grown? Would you therefore refrain from marrying? No, my daughters; for it is harder for me than for you, for the hand of the LORD has gone forth against me."

¹⁴And they lifted up their voices and wept again; and Orpah kissed her mother-in-law, but Ruth clung to her. ¹⁵Then she said, "Behold, your sister-in-law has gone back to her people and her gods; return after your sister-in-law." ¹⁶But Ruth said, "Do not urge me to leave you or turn back from following you; for where you go, I will go, and where you lodge, I will lodge. Your people shall be my people, and your God, my God. ¹⁷Where you die, I will die, and there I will be buried. Thus may the LORD do to me, and worse, if anything but death parts you and me." ¹⁸When she saw that she was determined to go with her, she said no more to her. ¹⁹So they both went until they came to Bethlehem. And when they had come to Bethlehem, all the city was stirred because of them, and the women said, "Is this Naomi?" ²⁰She said to them, "Do not call me Naomi; call me Mara, for the Almighty has dealt very bitterly with me. ²¹I went out full, but the LORD has brought me back empty. Why do you call me Naomi, since the LORD has witnessed against me and the Almighty has afflicted me?" ²²So Naomi returned, and with her Ruth the Moabitess, her daughter-in-law, who returned from the land of Moab. And they came to Bethlehem at the beginning of barley harvest.

–Ruth 1:6–22

CHAPTER THREE

THREE WIDOWS
THREE WAYS

Ruth 1:6–22

I have an aversion to doctors, dentists, and needles. Sit back in that dentist chair and the assistant comes in with a needle and promises, "This won't hurt a bit."

She lied.

On one occasion I had to drink something that could be tracked on a diagnostic machine. I was handed a glass containing a thick, gloppy, unappealing liquid. I hesitated. The doctor said, "Don't worry; it tastes like a milkshake."

It tasted like sludge.

I'm convinced that you can't get a medical degree without being able to lie with a straight face.

Several years ago, pain from a chipped tooth finally drove me to make that dreaded appointment with a dentist. I'd been taking pain relievers for months, and I finally knew I had to do something about it. I surrendered once again to the practice of medicine.

After taking x-rays of all my teeth, he informed me that I had not one but *three* broken teeth and would need three crowns.

I think *crown* is an appropriate term—given the fact that only kings and queens can afford them.

Nearly 200 years ago, Thomas Jefferson wrote a letter in which he stated to a friend, "The art of life is the avoiding of pain."[1]

That pretty well proves he stayed away from doctors, too.

But isn't the *real* art of life knowing how to respond to pain rather than how to avoid it?

According to Scripture, pain manufactures maturity. A crisis conditions character; difficulty develops depth.

The truth is difficulty and pain and suffering and sorrow create a cross-road experience: the path we choose to take will make all the difference in whether we grow and become sweeter or stagnate and become weaker in our faith.

If you've ever wondered where a crossroad experience is described in Scripture—where there were decisions to be made that would determine the destiny of a person's life—the first chapter of the Book of Ruth is such a place.

It is a crisis at the crossroad of life for three women following the death of their husbands. Their sorrow could not be avoided. Three graves would lead to a crisis of faith in the lives of these three widows.

And what a crisis it is.

All three had become a familiar sight at the local funeral home. The office staff knew Naomi by name. First, her husband died. Then one of her sons died, soon followed in death by the other.

No details . . . no description . . . just three widows grieving over their incredible loss. In their world and their culture, the loss of a husband was felt deeper than just the loss of companionship; the pain went deeper than sorrow. These deaths not only threatened their future happiness on earth but their ability to even survive.

Ten years earlier, Naomi, her husband, and their two sons had left Bethlehem believing they were leaving their troubles behind. Nothing but green pastures ahead. But now, ten years later, there is nothing in Moab for Naomi except three graves, great sorrow, and unbelievable grief.[2]

She can stay in Moab and mourn . . . and starve to death, or she can leave for home. Besides, word has reached her that Bethlehem has food again. Bethlehem, the House of Bread, has food for all who live there.

And without any apparent hesitation, Naomi **departed from the place where she was, and her two daughters-in-law with her; and they went on the way to return to the land of Judah** (Ruth 1:7).

It was a typical oriental custom for hosts to accompany their departing guests some distance down the road, then bid them farewell—which seems to be the picture here.[3]

These three widows eventually came to the border or, perhaps, the edge of the Jordan River just above the Dead Sea. Bethlehem was a three-day journey from Moab, and Naomi wouldn't have wanted them to walk very far before she bid them farewell, which is exactly what she had in mind:

> **And Naomi said to her two daughters-in-law, "Go, return each of you to her mother's house; may the LORD deal kindly with you as you have dealt with the dead and with me"** (Ruth 1:8).

You might think it strange for Naomi to encourage her daughters-in-law to return to their *mother's* house. This doesn't mean that Orpah and Ruth have deceased fathers. It actually refers to the mother's *place*; it was typically in the mother's bedchamber where marriages were planned and often arranged.[4]

Naomi is effectively saying, "Listen, girls, you're young; you have your life in front of you . . . go back to your mothers and makes plans for another wedding."

Naomi continues with her blessing:

> **"May the LORD grant that you may find rest, each in the house of her husband." Then she kissed them, and they lifted up their voices and wept** (Ruth 1:9).

Three widows' lives have been turned upside down by unfulfilled expectations and unexpected sorrows. There are few more tender and heartbreaking scenes in the Bible than this one.

Frankly, I've never met a family with three widows related to one another by marriage, where none have surviving children or grandchildren.

Without hope, security, or much of a future, they openly weep. This isn't one damsel in distress, but three. And here at the crossroad we are given a textbook lesson on three classic responses to pain, disillusionment, and sorrow.

Perhaps you can identify with one of these widows . . . perhaps, all three.

NAOMI AT THE CROSSROAD

You may remember that Naomi's name means *gracious one*; you could render it *pleasant* or, even, *sweet*. The problem is she has now become embittered—the lines in her face telling the story of three graves and great loss. When she eventually arrives back home, she'll refuse to be called by her given name.

She's concluded that she would best be left alone. Her advice to her daughters-in-law reveals the depth of her sorrow and resignation.

Unworthy of Love

Four times she will tell these young women to leave her alone and go back home. Her first reason for continuing the journey alone:

> **"Return, my daughters. Why should you go with me? Have I yet sons in my womb, that they may be your husbands?"**
> (Ruth 1:11).

In other words, "Since my sons are now gone, there's no longer any reason for you to be bound to me. There isn't anything in myself that is worthy of your following me or caring for me . . . I'm just an old woman now . . . surely you don't want to bother with me."

She continues:

> **"Return, my daughters! Go, for I am too old to have a husband. If I said I have hope, if I should even have a husband tonight and also bear sons, would you therefore wait until they were grown? Would you therefore refrain from marrying? No, my daughters, for it is harder for me than for you, for the hand of the LORD has gone forth against me"**
> (Ruth 1:12–13).

Peel back the layers of self-pity and she has convinced herself that God no longer loves her, either . . . why should Orpah or Ruth? Frankly, when you reach the point where you're convinced that God doesn't love you anymore, you're going to find it impossible to be loved by anybody else.

Loving God *and* believing God loves you forms a healthy foundation for both receiving love from others and giving love in return. Which means that genuine, self-sacrificing love is actually impossible apart from having first received the love of Jesus Christ.

David wrote,

> *Unless the Lord builds the house, they labor in vain who build it* (Psalm 127:1).

True love is a three-party transaction. The amazing, self-sacrificing commitment that Ruth will offer Naomi will be possible only because Ruth has *first* become committed to Naomi's God. The trouble is Naomi doesn't seem so convinced anymore that her God is worthy of being followed!

The second observation from Naomi's misguided advice is much more serious.

God Is Not Worthy of Worship

And they lifted up their voices and wept again; and Orpah kissed her mother-in-law, but Ruth clung to her. Then she said, "Behold, your sister-in-law has gone back to her people and her gods; return after your sister-in-law" (Ruth 1:14–15).

As tragic as it sounds, Naomi is actually encouraging these women to return to their families and their gods. She says:

- God's hand has been against me *(Ruth 1:13)*;
- God has dealt bitterly with me *(Ruth 1:20)*;
- God is against me and has afflicted me *(Ruth 1:21)*.

All that is saying, "My God has failed me; He's dropped the ball. Go on back to your gods—perhaps they'll treat you better."

What in the world is Naomi doing demanding that her daughters-in-law go back to their gods? Their chief god was Chemosh, and their worship included child sacrifice. Why would a Jewish woman—a daughter of Abraham—encourage two pagan women to worship their false gods?

One author suggested the possibility that Naomi wanted to go back to Bethlehem and she really didn't want anybody to know that she and her husband had permitted their two sons to marry pagan Gentiles.[5] In other words, this might have been an attempt to cover up her unfaithfulness to God.

If that was the case, two wrongs won't make anything right! In fact, she'll only be adding to her guilt.

In my opinion, Naomi isn't as interested in covering her unfaithful tracks as she is in revealing her unbelieving heart.

Naomi has concluded, "God isn't really worth following . . . I've been to the graveyard three times now, and it's obvious that God doesn't care."

Fast forward to the moment she arrives in Bethlehem:

> *And when they had come to Bethlehem, all the city was stirred because of them, and the women said, "Is this Naomi?"* (Ruth 1:19).

All Naomi's former friends and acquaintances come up to her and say, "Naomi, is that you?" She responds, ***"Do not call me Naomi; call me Mara"*** (Ruth 1:20*a*). That is, "Don't call me Pleasant anymore—call me Bitter, ***"for the Almighty has dealt very bitterly with me"*** (Ruth 1:20*b*). "*He* made me this way . . . it's all *His* fault."

Nowhere do you read of repentance for having abandoned God's covenant people and His covenant land. Frankly, Naomi is more interested in food than fellowship with God. She was returning to walk in her land, but she was *not* returning to walk with her Lord.

She continues:

> *"I went out full, but the LORD has brought me back empty"* (Ruth 1:21).

She's right, in a way—God has brought her *back*. She just doesn't realize at the moment that God hasn't deserted her, even though she has, effectively, deserted Him.

She has no idea that God *is* at work in her life now more than ever . . . that God has plans for a new son-in-law and a grandson named Obed, who will be the great-grandfather of King David.

We have the same problem. When suffering or sorrowing, we tend to magnify what we don't have and minimize what we do have. We tend to forget what God *did* when we're convinced there's something He should be *doing*.

But there is one ray of hope buried in her words: ***"We went out full and came back empty"*** (Ruth 1:21*a*). Note this—they left in the middle of a famine . . . they saw the devaluation of their property . . . enemy Midianites were lurking on the borders. That's why they headed for the green and fertile fields of Moab!

But notice what she admitted to these young widows: ".When we left Bethlehem we were, in reality, *full*. We had everything that really mattered back home in Bethlehem." Yes, they did!

ORPAH AT THE CROSSROAD

When Naomi first demanded that the girls return to their mothers, both Ruth and Orpah refused to go, and they said in unison, ***"We will surely return with you to your people"*** (Ruth 1:10).

But then Naomi lays out the reality of what they'll lose if they do. And for Orpah, that will change everything.

Naomi promised Orpah that:

- her life will be difficult as a widow from Moab;

- her prospects for a husband will be less than nothing;

- she will be unwanted by the Jewish community (Moabites and Jews don't get along—in fact, they hated one another);

- she will leave her nation with all its comfortable customs and conditions for a foreign country;

- she will forfeit her rights as a citizen;

- she is given no prospects and no promises.

And Orpah wept, kissed her mother-in-law, and said goodbye.

J. Vernon McGee wrote that Ruth and Orpah demonstrate two kinds of members in the church: the *professors* and the *possessors*. Orpah made a profession of faith, but Ruth possessed genuine faith.[6]

At this crossroad of life, a decision is made by Orpah which will determine her eternal destiny.

There are many like her who believe Christ will interrupt their lives more than they would find acceptable—God will foul up their social connections and reputation—Christ won't provide the needed prospects and guarantees—they might have to give up an idol or two. In fact, following Christ might even mean bearing a cross.

So Orpah calculated the cost and decided to go back to darkness. She was sad about it and she shed real tears. But, at this crossroad of life, she chooses to go back to paganism . . . back to Moab . . . back to her gods. And this time, her marriage will be to a man of Moabite stock.

Orpah disappears over the horizon, and she's never mentioned again in the Bible.

You can almost see Naomi turning to Ruth and saying, "Well, what are you waiting for? ***Behold, your sister-in-law has gone back to her people and her gods; return after your sister-in-law*** (Ruth 1:15). Go on . . . *get* . . . *shoo!*"

But what happens next is nothing less than one of the greatest confessions of faith you'll find anywhere in Scripture.

RUTH AT THE CROSSROAD

> ***But Ruth said, "Do not urge me to leave you or turn back from following you; for where you go, I will go, and where you lodge, I will lodge. Your people shall be my people, and your God, my God. Where you die, I will die, and there I will be buried. Thus may the LORD do to me, and worse, if anything but death parts you and me." When she saw that she was determined to go with her, she said no more to her*** (Ruth 1:16–18).

In summary, Ruth tells Naomi that no matter what the future holds and no matter where their future takes them, she will stay by her side. This is no snap decision—no whim or sudden impulse. Ruth knows that Naomi has nothing to offer her except poverty and hardship.

She has absolutely nothing to gain by going with Naomi . . . and she has everything to lose.[7] The most remote thing in her future is the sound of wedding bells.

Naomi tried to tell her to go back to her mother, implying that Ruth's mother, a Moabitess, is evidently alive. But can you imagine the conversation if Ruth went back? "Ruth, are you out of your mind?! I knew there would be trouble when you married that Israelite. Now stay in Moab; stick to your family . . . worship our gods . . . and for goodness' sake, marry a nice Moabite man!"

We've read this story so often that we've forgotten what Ruth is giving up. She's already lost her husband. Now she's turning her back on her citizenship, her country, her family, her religion, and her security.

She is literally giving away her future.

One author put it this way:

> Ruth possesses nothing. No deity has promised her blessing; no human being has come to her aid. She lives and chooses without a support system, and she knows that the fruit of her decision may well be the emptiness of rejection and, perhaps, even death. She has committed herself to an older widow rather than search for a new husband. There is no more radical decision in all the memories of Israel.[8]

Twice in this well-rehearsed speech, she refers to God in personal terminology. The God of Israel is now *her* God.

While in Toulon, France, a number of years ago, Marsha and I stayed with Pastor John-Pierre and his wife Jocelyn. John-Pierre couldn't speak English very well and Jocelyn often translated for him as we talked together.

One evening, John-Pierre told us about a young lady who had recently received Christ. She faced a great deal of persecution due to her decision. She had lost her friends and was nearly disowned by her family. Then John-Pierre said something that Jocelyn was having a hard time translating into English. She finally said, "My husband is saying that in spite of everything, this young lady *gripped God*."

She gripped, by faith, her living Lord. Sounds a lot like Ruth.

Here are three widows with three different ways of handling the pain of life that they just couldn't avoid.

Orpah departs—her shallow faith based on circumstances.

Naomi returns—her weak faith biased by circumstances.

And Ruth arrives—her new faith seeing beyond circumstances.

Heading for a strange new land, she has a tight grip on her true and living God.

Now Naomi had a kinsman of her husband, a man of great wealth, of the family of Elimelech, whose name was Boaz. ²*And Ruth the Moabitess said to Naomi, "Please let me go to the field and glean among the ears of grain after one in whose sight I may find favor." And she said to her, "Go, my daughter."* ³*So she departed and went and gleaned in the field after the reapers; and she happened to come to the portion of the field belonging to Boaz, who was of the family of Elimelech.* ⁴*Now behold, Boaz came from Bethlehem and said to the reapers, "May the LORD be with you." And they said to him, "May the LORD bless you."* ⁵*Then Boaz said to his servant who was in charge of the reapers, "Whose young woman is this?"* ⁶*The servant in charge of the reapers replied, "She is the young Moabite woman who returned with Naomi from the land of Moab.* ⁷*And she said, 'Please let me glean and gather after the reapers among the sheaves.' Thus she came and has remained from the morning until now; she has been sitting in the house for a little while."*

⁸*Then Boaz said to Ruth, "Listen carefully, my daughter. Do not go to glean in another field; furthermore, do not go on from this one, but stay here with my maids.* ⁹*Let your eyes be on the field which they reap, and go after them. Indeed, I have commanded the servants not to touch you. When you are thirsty, go to the water jars and drink from what the servants draw."* ¹⁰*Then she fell on her face, bowing to the ground and said to him, "Why have I found favor in your sight that you should take notice of me, since I am a foreigner?"* ¹¹*Boaz replied to her, "All that you have done for your mother-in-law after the death of your husband has been fully reported to me, and how you left your father and your mother and the land of your birth, and came to a people that you did not previously know.* ¹²*May the LORD reward your work, and your wages be full from the LORD, the God of Israel, under whose wings you have come to seek refuge."* ¹³*Then she said, "I have found favor in your sight, my lord, for you have comforted me and indeed have spoken kindly to your maidservant, though I am not like one of your maidservants."*

–Ruth 2:1–13

CHAPTER FOUR

NO SUCH THING AS CHANCE

Ruth 2:1–13

In the last chapter I poked fun at the medical profession because things they tell us might not be, well, exactly true. Needles don't just sting—they hurt! I've actually been told the inside story by friends in that field; if they told us the real story, we wouldn't like that, either.

A middle-aged man went for a routine physical. The nurse came in to update his medical information. She asked him, "How much do you weigh?" He said, "Oh, about 165." Somewhat suspicious, the nurse had him step on the digital scale and then said, "*Hmmm*, you weigh 210 pounds, to be exact."

She then asked him, "How tall are you?" He said, "About six feet." She looked him over and then asked him to step up to a measuring chart posted on the wall. "Well, you're actually 5 feet 8½ inches tall," the nurse reported.

She took his blood pressure and then gasped, "Sir, your blood pressure is extremely high!" "High!" he said, "What'd you expect? When I came in here I was tall and lanky, and you've just informed me I'm short and fat."

That's not funny, is it?!

For those of you in the medical profession, you have a really tough job, and we're actually proud of you and the work you do. Keep telling us the truth . . . even if it really does hurt.

By the time you finish the first chapter in the Book of Ruth, you're probably wondering if it contains any good news. It's been one piece of bad news after another, so far. And the news has been brutal.

Apart from Ruth's commitment to Naomi, this drama is a tragedy worthy of Shakespeare. Two widows have returned to Bethlehem—one a foreigner and the other, a woman who once had status in the community and respect throughout Bethlehem. Now, she's destitute and impoverished. She expects to spend the rest of her life living on handouts.

Chapter two is where it all begins to turn around. In fact, it will cover the events of only twenty-four hours, but what a day it will be.

Keep in mind that these are the days of the judges. There is no record of priest or prophet to provide biblical counsel. These aren't easy days for spiritually minded men and virtuous women to succeed.

The odds are stacked against them.

When we finish chapter two, most people may come to the conclusion that luck must have happened by. In fact, the world would consider Ruth and Boaz *lucky* and the events surrounding their meeting amazing *coincidences*. The truth is for a believer living in any generation, any culture, there are no coincidences—there is no such thing as chance.

This chapter will reveal the invisible hand of God in the midst of ordinary, everyday decisions. There are no voices from heaven . . . no messages from angelic visitors . . . no visible signs reassuring them.

This chapter is the personification of *Proverbs 3:5–6*:

> *Trust in the LORD with all your heart and do not lean on your own understanding. In all your ways acknowledge Him, and He will make your paths straight.*

And that's exactly what will happen here.

It opens with Samuel giving us the slightest of hints that an amazing solution for Ruth and Naomi is just ahead:

> **Now Naomi had a kinsman of her husband, a man of great wealth, of the family of Elimelech, whose name was Boaz** (Ruth 2:1).

With this brief statement, the author builds anticipation and hope by hinting to us that we've probably just been introduced to the future kinsman redeemer—the knight in shining armor.

We're also given in this opening verse several glimpses into the life and character of Boaz; in short, verse one is a biography loaded with a volume of implications.

A BRIEF BIOGRAPHY OF BOAZ

Boaz Is Clearly Related to Naomi

The Hebrew word for *kinsman* can refer both to a personal friend *or* a relative. We'll confirm later in this chapter that he is a close relative. According to rabbinical tradition passed down through the centuries, Boaz was believed to be a nephew of Elimelech, Naomi's deceased husband.[1]

Boaz is thus qualified to become a potential redeemer of Elimelech's estate, which could rescue *both* Naomi and Ruth from destitution and poverty.

Boaz Is Greatly Respected in Bethlehem

Ruth 2:1 also informs us that Boaz is **a man of great wealth**. This Hebrew phrase is difficult to define. The same Hebrew word is translated *valiant warrior* in *Joshua 6:2* and *mighty man of war* in *2 Samuel 17:8*.

When the angel of God came to Gideon in *Judges 6* and said, *"The Lord is with you, O valiant warrior,"* he used the same adjective.

The term has such a strong military context that some scholars believe Boaz was a veteran soldier.

Since Boaz lived in the days of Gideon, he would have been an eligible soldier when Gideon called for faithful men to volunteer from among the tribes. Some Old Testament scholars go so far as to suggest that Boaz was one of Gideon's 300 valiant men.

The adjective can mean much more than valiant warrior. In fact, it's translated in *1 Samuel 9:1 a man of influence*. The same expression actually appears again in **Ruth 3:11**, when Boaz tells Ruth that she is **a woman of excellence**. Finally, the word is clearly used to refer to a man of great wealth in *2 Kings 15:20*.[2]

Typically, the context will help determine which of these nuances the Spirit of God intended as a description. More than likely, given the poverty of Ruth who comes to glean in the fields of Boaz, the wealth of this Israelite landowner is the most critical piece of knowledge—at least, for now.

This was another way of saying with only one adjective that Boaz could completely eliminate the poverty of these two widows, should he choose to do so.

Boaz was actually all the above: a man of honor, integrity, influence and, certainly, wealth. In fact, every one of these attributes will be demonstrated throughout the remainder of this true-to-life fairytale.

There is one additional quality to the godly character of Boaz that could easily be overlooked.

Boaz Is Spiritually Reassuring to His Employees

You can't help but notice what happens when Boaz first arrives at his fields where his employees are hard at work:

> ***Now behold, Boaz came from Bethlehem and said to the reapers, "May the LORD be with you." And they said to him, "May the LORD bless you"*** (Ruth 2:4).

Don't skip over this greeting. Boaz arrives and immediately shows concern well beyond the normal greeting of *Shalom* (Peace to you). His words both greeted them and gave them his personal wish for them. Look again: ***May the LORD be with you.***

In other words, Boaz is saying to his employees that he wants them to not only be blessed but blessed by the sense that Yahweh was with them— blessing their work . . . blessing their lives.[3]

Can you imagine a boss at work passing by an employee's desk and saying, "I hope you sense the presence of God today as you work"!

Do you have anyone working under your supervision? Why not make it your goal this week to say something to let them know you want God's blessing on their lives. You might receive an empty stare in return; you might see that employee tear up and say, "No one has ever cared about me in that way before."

Or you could end up with a warning from the front office that you're being too open about your religion.

You may be tempted to think, *But this is Boaz. He knows he's going to be in the Bible one day.*

No, he doesn't.

This isn't religious jargon, and he has no idea Samuel will write about him one day. Boaz actually means it. And his employees know that, too. And they respond in like manner by saying, "And may God bless you."

Don't forget: these are the days when Israel's morals were at an all-time low; people have lived spiritually defeated lives for nearly a decade. They are raw with physical needs, as well, since the famine is in the recent past.

Boaz just so happens to care about more than a bumper crop. He cares about these peasants scraping out an existence with their bare hands.

On the canvass of Scripture, the portrait of Boaz is painted with the brush strokes of integrity, honesty, humility, diligence, godly character, and concern for others.

These may very well have been the reasons he was still single. He probably wasn't all that interesting to the local girls. They wanted his money, but there was no interest in his desire to connect people to the providence of God; to them, he probably talked about God *way* too much. And Boaz wasn't interested in settling for someone of lesser character and trivial interests.

These were the days of the judges *where everyone did that which was right in his own eyes* (Judges 21:25). In a culture marked by moral and spiritual decadence, Boaz and Ruth are going to shine with unbelievably distinctive character and integrity.

But before Ruth begins to glean in the fields of Boaz, let's stop and glean some gems from this biography of the man.

It's Possible to Have a Passionate Interest in God, Even When Most People Have Forgotten Him

Imagine, in the midst of this self-serving generation, a wealthy man will ride out to his fields and bring the name of his God to the ears and minds of every employee; he greets everyone in the name of his LORD. His tribesmen might have lost their conviction that God was worth following, but not Boaz.

His *first* recorded words reveal nothing less than a passionate belief that God is not only worth following—He is worth talking about and thinking about during a hard day's work in the fields of wheat and barley.

And so Boaz greets his world with, "Listen, God is not only worth following, but I hope you actually sense His presence as you work in the fields today."

It's Possible to Be Self-Sacrificing, Even When the Culture around You Is Self-Serving

This was a time when everyone did whatever *they* wanted to do; it was a dog-eat-dog world. Yet Boaz was a man who cared about people—the poorest of people in the lowest class of society.

The Law of Moses dictated that farmers must leave the corners of their fields for the poor to glean. It also prescribed that gleaners had the right to come along and pick up what was accidentally left behind *(Leviticus 19:9–10)*.

But these were tough times! In these days, throughout Israel, farmers would refuse to follow the Law of Moses. They would forbid the presence of gleaners; in fact, they would send their own farm hands back into the fields to gather what was accidently dropped or left behind.

I mean, who in their right mind would follow God's laws of generosity and mercy in times like these?

Boaz would. And because he would, he will soon meet Ruth.

Boaz will care for the needs of those who were thrown out of other fields. And because Boaz accepted the burden of the Law's requirements, he will actually discover his bride-to-be. Isn't that just great?!

> **And Ruth the Moabitess said to Naomi, "Please let me go to the field and glean among the ears of grain after one in whose sight I may find favor." And she said to her, "Go, my daughter." So she departed and went and gleaned in the field after the reapers** (Ruth 2:2–3a).

In Bible times, the reaper would grab a few stalks with one hand and cut off the grain with a short sickle held in the other hand. They would hold on to those stalks, grab a few more, and cut them off with quick strokes, eventually filling their hand with a bundle of stalks. The reaper would then either tie the stalks together or lay them down for other workers who would come along and tie them and stack them on carts.

The reapers worked carefully. They weren't in the habit of leaving stalks behind. For the poor gleaners foraging in the field, finding fallen and abandoned stalks of grain would have been rare; living off gleaning would have been as difficult as trying to sell cast off aluminum cans to recycling centers. And the greedier the farmer, the less likely a gleaner would find anything left behind.

By the grace and providence of God, Ruth *just so happened* to choose the fields of Boaz to begin foraging for their next meal:

> **And she happened to come to the portion of the field belonging to Boaz, who was of the family of Elimelech** (Ruth 2:3*b*).

The Hebrew language literally reads, "She chanced to chance upon the field."[4]

Samuel must have been smiling as he wrote the obvious play on words to imply that what the world might have considered a coincidence was nothing less than Divine Providence.

There were no lights flashing; no band playing out in Boaz's field; no voice was instructing, "Ruth, turn left and go through that gate!"[5] To Ruth, it was just an ordinary decision: *I think I'll go in this man's field right here and start gleaning over there in that corner.*

To the world it was blind chance. The believer knows better. Our hearts are immediately awed by the wonder of God's silent provocation . . . the subtle stirrings of the Spirit that moved Ruth's feet through the gate of Boaz's field.

This is *Proverbs 3:6* in living color: *In all your ways acknowledge Him and He shall direct your paths* (NKJV).

A coincidence? Not a chance!

My wife and I enjoy hearing the testimonies of how couples met each other for the first time . . . how God arranged the details of that initial meeting. It reveals nothing less than the creative glory of God's providence. And is He ever creative!

A missionary pioneer told me how God introduced him to his future wife. He was attending the same college that she did, but they had never met. As he prepared to graduate that spring, another young lady gave him the name and address of a girl her brother had dated. She highly recommended that he look her up; her character and charm were worth pursuing. Paul stuck the piece of paper in his wallet and then completely forgot about it.

Two years later, he was preaching in meetings around the country as an evangelist when, one night, he decided to clean out his wallet. He discovered that little piece of paper. Paul couldn't help but wonder if Betty had ever married.

On a whim, he wrote a letter, asking her if she'd be interested in meeting him in the future. When his letter arrived, she had just returned from a Christian workers conference where she had committed her life to full-time Christian service. She wrote him back and said, "Yes, I'd be happy to meet you."

Eventually, this young man had a couple of preaching opportunities near her hometown. He *just so happened* to arrive in town the day World War II ended and, as a result, a two-day national holiday was declared by the U.S. government.

Paul's meetings were cancelled as the country celebrated her returning troops and rest from years of war. Obviously Paul had nothing to do for the next few days and Betty's father *just so happened* to invite him to stay at their home.

Two months later, Paul and Betty Jane Freed were married.

Paul went on to serve as the president of Trans World Radio for many decades; both he and Betty Jane joined our fellowship when we were still meeting as a young church plant at East Cary Middle School. Their vision for the world and their passion for the Gospel of Jesus Christ impacted my early years as a pastor and served to help formulate and foster a vision to reach a lost world for the glory of God. I am forever indebted to the testimony of their marriage, their pioneering spirit in ministry, and their loyal friendship.

Like Boaz and Ruth, they are proof that guidance from the Lord is promised, but it often comes on the heels of *ordinary* decisions and circumstances beyond our control.

In all our lives, there are no bands playing or signs flashing, either. But when your heart surrenders to this kindred Spirit, when your mind and will declare the same things Ruth's did—that the God of Israel will be *my* God— ordinary decisions will do nothing more than move your feet to the right gate and focus your eyes on the right field.

David said it this way: *The steps of a good man are ordered by the LORD* (Psalm 37:23 KJV).

Ruth is now gleaning in the fields of a potential redeemer. And wouldn't you know it—Boaz *just so happened* to come visiting those fields that very morning:

> **Now behold, Boaz came from Bethlehem and said to the reapers, "May the LORD be with you." And they said to him, "May the LORD bless you"** (Ruth 2:4).

And is He ever about to!

At this moment, Boaz spotted Ruth:

> **Then Boaz said to his servant who was in charge of the reapers, "Whose young woman is this?"** (Ruth 2:5).

This is the Hebrew equivalent to "Wow . . . who is *that*?!" It's almost the same thing as spotting a pretty girl and letting out a whistle.

I remember whistling that way to my older daughter when she was around four years old. She didn't know what that particular whistle meant, and I wanted her to know it ahead of time. I said, "Honey, one of these days some young man will drive up next to you, roll down his window and whistle just like that in your direction. It means he thinks you're pretty and he wants your attention. So, when he does that, spit in his window and run home to Daddy!"

That's not likely.

After Boaz catches his breath, his servant responds to his query:

> **"She is the young Moabite woman who returned with Naomi from the land of Moab. And she said, 'Please let me glean and gather after the reapers among the sheaves.' Thus she came and has remained from the morning until now; she has been sitting in the house for a little while"** (Ruth 2:6–7).

Let's slow down for just a moment. We're about to watch as Boaz goes into the house to meet Ruth. Can you imagine that first encounter? We'll discover later that Boaz knows he's a potential redeemer, but Ruth doesn't.

His heart is pounding as he walks inside that house. He's already mapping out an immediate plan to get her attention. She'll carry home more grain than any reaper in Israel's history. In the meantime, he walks through the door, clears his throat, and introduces himself.

It's not so different from today. Meeting that girl you were interested in takes some strategy, especially if you want to ask her for a date. And that can be nothing less than terrifying!

Someone said that it's like handing her a loaded gun that's pointing directly at your heart, and then asking, "Will you go out with me?" If she answers no, it's like pulling the trigger. If she says yes, there is life to live and joy to feel!

I remember asking my future bride for that first date. Of all things, I asked her if I could take her to a church service. How's that for irony? She's just about *lived* at church ever since.

I see Boaz carefully creating his opening speech . . . and it's a thing of beauty!

> **Then Boaz said to Ruth, "Listen carefully, my daughter. Do not go to glean in another field; furthermore, do not go on from this one, but stay here with my maids. Let your eyes be on the field which they reap, and go after them. Indeed, I have commanded the servants not to touch you. When you are thirsty, go to the water jars and drink from what the servants draw"** (Ruth 2:8–9).

Boaz has virtually considered every conceivable way to make sure Ruth gleans only in his field. She is given permission to follow freely behind the reapers; she's invited to drink from the company water cooler—which means she won't have to walk back into town if she runs out of water; she'll be offered a free meal, as well.

Did you notice that Boaz has *already* commanded his men not to touch Ruth. This phrase can refer to physically injuring her. The truth is they wouldn't have wanted any competition for fallen grain . . . who is this foreign woman anyway!

The phrase can also be translated to sexually molest *(Genesis 20:6)*. Ruth is a young woman, without friends, all alone, vulnerable, a foreigner without legal protection. She would have been an easy target to manipulate . . . or harm . . . or worse.

And who in all of Israel would even care, which is why Boaz has effectively told everyone, "*I* am now her *guardian*—don't get in her way, don't lay a hand on her, give her water to drink when she wants it, and watch out for her."

No wonder we're told that in response to these remarks from Boaz, Ruth *fell on her face, bowing to the ground* [an Old Testament form of courtesy] *and said to him, "Why have I found favor in your sight that you should take notice of me, since I am a foreigner?"* (Ruth 2:10).

Now remember, Ruth doesn't know Boaz is related to Naomi. Boaz knows. At this moment, Ruth only knows that this wealthy landowner is showing extreme kindness to her, and she can't quite figure out why.

Boaz proceeds to tell her that he actually knows quite a bit about her testimony:

> *"All that you have done for your mother-in-law after the death of your husband has been fully reported to me, and how you left your father and your mother and the land of your birth, and came to a people that you did not previously know"* (Ruth 2:11).

Boaz says, in effect, "Ruth, I already know everything about what you've been through: the death of your husband, your commitment to Naomi and to the God of Abraham, your sacrifice of service to Naomi, your conversion to Israel's Sovereign Lord, and your willingness to leave your family and your security for a new land and a new people without any guarantee of survival."

Boaz is saying, "You have something special on the inside that is worth protecting and even honoring."

I love what Boaz says next:

> *"May the LORD reward your work, and your wages be full from the LORD, the God of Israel, under whose wings you have come to seek refuge"* (Ruth 2:12).

Did this guy walk with God, or what?!

Why hasn't the Church heard more about Boaz? Why aren't there books written for men on the life and character of Boaz? This man's brief appearance in Scripture is deeply convicting to every man who encounters his perspective, his actions, his character, and his purity.

He and Ruth have only recently met and, again, he's already talking about God. And he's doing more than just dropping God's name—he's advocating for God; he's actually entrusting her to God and praying that God will bless her.

Boaz is effectively saying here, "Ruth, I happen to know that you've left family, friends, and country. I know you're probably afraid and somewhat lonely. So listen, dear girl, just come close and snuggle up under the wings of Almighty God and rest assured that He will watch over you; He's trustworthy. In fact, I'm going to pray that He will repay your deeds with kindness."

Boaz could have proposed right then and there! He will . . . in due time.

Before we get too far ahead of ourselves, there are two principles to note from this initial encounter between Boaz and Ruth:

1. The foundation for a romantic relationship is a vital relationship with Jesus Christ.

Let me speak candidly to every single person who's read this far: if that guy or girl you're interested in walks with God, it will not take you very long to confirm it. But if, after one date, their acknowledgement of God and the things of God don't resonate loud and clear—whether it's wanting to pray before eating a meal or making references to the Lord, the Bible, or church—take off . . . see them disappear from your rear-view mirror!

Throughout my years of shepherding, I have warned countless individuals. The person they described to me as evidencing little spiritual interest and less desire to walk with Christ was providing *plenty* of warning signs that trouble and sorrow were in the making.

I've dealt with far too many people on the other side of marriage who refused to run; who lowered their standard; who made concessions; who compromised in their choices apart from prayer and obedience to Scripture—brokenhearted people who thought it would be better to marry an uncommitted Christian, or even a non-Christian, rather than to remain single.

Encouragement and wisdom for them is a different subject and another book; for the moment my warning is for those who stand on the shore of singlehood and truly wish to be sailing at sea. Dear friend, it is far better to remain on shore and wish to be sailing, than sailing and wish you were still on shore. In the meantime, your greatest protection from commitment to the wrong person is the principle I've just discussed: if their relationship with Christ isn't real, don't move ahead toward romance.

You can bank on this next principle:

2.   A permanent attraction between a man and a woman should go beyond the physical dimension to include the spiritual.

Decades ago, I wanted to ask Marsha—that young lady who sat in my college English classroom—for a date, and it took me all semester to work up the nerve.

Her beautiful blue eyes turned me into jello. I'd never had a conversation with her. I'd never heard her testimony . . . I sure hoped she had one. But beyond that first date and her blue eyes, it would be a spiritual connection—a spiritual dimension—that would matter most.

J. Vernon McGee pointed out a fact in his commentary on Ruth that is easily missed. He said that *nowhere* in the Book of Ruth are we told what Ruth looked like—not one physical description is given, not even the color of her eyes.[6]

Boaz was smitten by her, no doubt . . . but what ultimately attracted this very eligible bachelor to Ruth was her commitment to God and her character of godliness.

This encounter in a Bethlehem field was not by chance; it was not a coincidence. God had been developing separately two lives that in a matter of months would become one heart, one home, one spirit, one path.

Two people were acknowledging God in all their ways, and God was directing their paths . . . together.

¹⁴*At mealtime Boaz said to her, "Come here, that you may eat of the bread and dip your piece of bread in the vinegar." So she sat beside the reapers; and he served her roasted grain, and she ate and was satisfied and had some left. ¹⁵When she rose to glean, Boaz commanded his servants, saying, "Let her glean even among the sheaves, and do not insult her. ¹⁶Also you shall purposely pull out for her some grain from the bundles and leave it that she may glean, and do not rebuke her."*

¹⁷*So she gleaned in the field until evening. Then she beat out what she had gleaned, and it was about an ephah of barley. ¹⁸She took it up and went into the city, and her mother-in-law saw what she had gleaned. She also took it out and gave Naomi what she had left after she was satisfied. ¹⁹Her mother-in-law then said to her, "Where did you glean today and where did you work? May he who took notice of you be blessed." So she told her mother-in-law with whom she had worked and said, "The name of the man with whom I worked today is Boaz." ²⁰Naomi said to her daughter-in-law, "May he be blessed of the LORD who has not withdrawn his kindness to the living and to the dead." Again Naomi said to her, "The man is our relative, he is one of our closest relatives." ²¹Then Ruth the Moabitess said, "Furthermore, he said to me, 'You should stay close to my servants until they have finished all my harvest.'" ²²Naomi said to Ruth her daughter-in-law, "It is good, my daughter, that you go out with his maids, so that others do not fall upon you in another field." ²³So she stayed close by the maids of Boaz in order to glean until the end of the barley harvest and the wheat harvest. And she lived with her mother-in-law.*

–Ruth 2:14–23

CHAPTER FIVE

GLEANING IN THE FIELDS OF GRACE

Ruth 2:14–23

The *Wisconsin State Journal* interviewed several personnel managers of some of the nation's largest corporations and asked for their most unusual experiences interviewing prospective employees, and here is a sampling of the results:

- The interviewer was challenged to arm wrestle—as if that had anything to do with getting the job.
- Another wore earphones and the interviewer could hear music playing. When asked to remove them, the applicant explained it was no problem because he could listen to the interviewer and the music at the same time.
- A baldheaded applicant suddenly excused himself and then came back a few minutes later, wearing a full toupee. Evidently he'd left it in his car.
- A young woman said she'd not had time to eat her lunch before arriving and promptly began devouring her hamburger and fries as the interview commenced.
- Another actually dozed off during his interview.
- Strangely bizarre was the guy who explained that he'd never actually finished high school because he had been kidnapped and kept alive in a closet in Mexico.

Needless to say, none of the above landed the jobs they wanted.[1]

Grace has it limits. Besides, when it comes to getting the job you believe you deserve, it really doesn't have anything to do with *grace*. It has everything to do with earning the job you get.

For the average Christian who picks up the Book of Ruth, one of our problems in appreciating the sheer beauty of God's grace in her life is assuming everything that happens to her is something she *deserved*:

- why, of course, she ends up in the fields of Boaz,

- and he's immediately smitten with her,

- and takes pity on her,

- and obviously treats her with kindness.

She deserved every bit of it, right? Actually, she deserves none of the favor Boaz will show her. She is an outsider, a foreigner, a former idolater, and a destitute widow with absolutely nothing to offer him . . . except gratitude.

This is the rich truth of God's grace. Grace is undeserved, unmerited favor. Grace is God's condescension to us, not because we deserve it, but because He is gracious. Grace is God choosing us, not because we were the best applicant for the job, at the head of the class, or superior to all others . . . far from it.

The Apostle Paul spelled it out:

> *But God, being rich in mercy, because of His great love with which He loved us, even when we were dead in our transgressions, made us alive together with Christ . . . so that in the ages to come He might show the surpassing riches of His grace in kindness toward us in Christ Jesus* (Ephesians 2:4–5, 7).

What we are about to witness in the fields of Bethlehem is nothing less than a demonstration of grace—sheer, glorious kindness toward someone entirely unlikely and, certainly, undeserving.

Ruth is gleaning in the fields of grace.

At least six principles of grace will be played out in flesh and blood between Boaz—an illustration of Christ—and Ruth—an illustration of the believer, the Bride of Christ.

GRACE TAKES THE INITIATIVE
AND MAKES THE FIRST MOVE

Notice it is Boaz who speaks first to Ruth. With kindness he says:

"Listen carefully, my daughter. Do not go to glean in another field; furthermore, do not go on from this one, but stay here with my maids. Let your eyes be on the field which they reap, and go after them. Indeed, I have commanded the servants not to touch you. When you are thirsty, go to the water jars and drink from what the servants draw" (Ruth 2:8–9).

In this culture Boaz is obviously acting with grace toward the less worthy Ruth, a foreign widow who, as a reaper, occupied the lowest rung on the ladder of society.

My wife and I had the privilege of seeing some of the sights throughout London and Scotland a couple of years ago. We saw several palaces of Queen Elizabeth II and were told that whenever the queen was in residence, her flag would be flying above the palace. We arrived at one palace and stood outside a massive, gated entrance. It was locked, of course, but that didn't keep me from trying the handle. So we simply stood there looking through the iron grating toward the elaborate castle several hundred feet away. We knew the queen was in—we saw her flag flying above the palace roof.

Just imagine Queen Elizabeth suddenly appearing at the castle door, waving at us, and then coming over to the gate to shake our hands, saying, "I decided to venture out here and have a chat with you straightaway."

That wouldn't happen; it would be a massive breach of protocol. The queen doesn't chat with tourists standing outside her gate. Maybe a wave . . . a nod from the balcony . . . but that would be it.

A senator received a phone call from the newly elected President of the United States; assuming it was a prank, she hung up on him. He called her back and introduced himself again. She hung up again, still thinking it was a gag. I watched her being interviewed on television later and she laughed, "The President of the United States doesn't call *me!*"

Who would expect a call from the president? Who would anticipate a conversation with the Queen of England? Not unless you've done something to deserve it—perhaps, something heroic.

We take for granted this stunning announcement: [God,] *in these last days has spoken to us in His Son* (Hebrews 1:2).

Grace is God speaking to unworthy, less than heroic peasants, and it was illustrated for us centuries before the coming of Christ when Boaz spoke to Ruth. That conversation was no less remarkable in their culture than if the queen talked to us at her palace gate or if the president called our home.

GRACE SURPRISES US WITH PROVISION AND PROTECTION

Now after Boaz rehearses to Ruth what he will provide for her, the first words in response to him were disbelief. She simply can't believe his kindness. She can't comprehend his care.

In fact, don't miss the first word she ever says to Boaz in their very first conversation: ***"Why?!"*** Yes, she wonders why he is doing this for her.

Recipients of grace are usually surprised—they know more than anyone that they are undeserving. Ruth didn't respond to Boaz saying, "I knew I'd catch your eye . . . I knew you'd single me out . . . I've been expecting your generous help."

Far from it. I am fairly convinced that when we arrive in heaven and gasp at the splendor of His preparation on our behalf and begin to grasp our eternal role as the Bride of Christ, we will kneel at the feet of our Boaz, and probably ask, "Why?"

Why would the King do all this for me? The answer is—grace. And the recipient is left speechless as kindness dawns, scattering the shadows of unbelief.

> *Amazing grace! How sweet the sound*
> *That saved a wretch like me!*
> *I once was lost, but now am found;*
> *Was blind, but now I see.*[2]

GRACE IS WILLING TO PLAY THE ROLE OF SERVANT TO SOMEONE LESS WORTHY

There is a lapse in time between this first conversation in verse 13 and what happens next in verse 14. Ruth evidently goes off to spend the rest of the morning gleaning in the fields, no doubt stunned by this incredibly kind landowner.

But before long, it's time for lunch. As instructed, Ruth sits near enough to get water to drink, perhaps munching on the raw grain she's already gathered—if she eats anything at all.

Boaz has been watching for just this moment . . . the timing was perfect:

> *At mealtime Boaz said to her, "Come here, that you may eat of the bread and dip your piece of bread in the vinegar"* (Ruth 2:14*a*).

This implies Ruth doesn't have any bread of her own and Boaz is asking her to eat with him. You could call this their first date; the open fields of Boaz were the original Outback restaurant.

Okay, so it was a group date . . . but it was a start.

Don't take this moment for granted. Ruth would have been amazed all over again; a gleaner was one step away from begging on the street corner. In fact, reapers were so poor that a satisfactory meal was an unexpected blessing.[3]

Ruth was invited to take some of their bread and dip it into a vinegar-based sauce that was customary for this culture.

But then it gets even better:

> *So she sat beside the reapers; and he served her roasted grain, and she ate and was satisfied and had some left* (Ruth 2:14*b*).

From his own skillet he knelt down and, as was their custom, brushed some roasted kernels onto her mat or into her lap. Did their eyes meet? Did they both blush from the obvious knowledge of this spontaneous kindness?

You'd better believe it.

The other reapers and Boaz's employees are watching every moment and probably wondering if they ought to slip away and leave these two alone!

Ruth eats and then, the text implies, she rose to go back to gleaning while the rest of the employees were still resting. It's possible that she was a bit too embarrassed by the curious looks and the wondering glances cast in her direction.

Nobody had missed that moment when Boaz the prince treated a servant girl as if she were a member of his closest circle of friends. The prince had taken the role of a servant and stooped to serve an impoverished widow.

That's grace.

GRACE WORKS BEHIND THE SCENES TO PROVIDE FOR THE OBJECT OF ITS AFFECTION

As soon as Ruth gets up and leaves, Boaz has more surprises for his stunned friends and co-workers:

> **When she rose** [that is, left] **to glean, Boaz commanded his servants, saying, "Let her glean even among the sheaves, and do not insult her. Also you shall purposely pull out for her some grain from the bundles and leave it that she may glean, and do not rebuke her** (Ruth 2:15–16).

Okay, this is *not* normal behavior. Was Boaz actually telling his team of reapers to throw grain in her path?[4]

Yes!

They were probably thinking, *C'mon Boaz, just ask her to marry you; it'll be easier on all of us. Get it over with!*

One can only imagine Ruth continuing to glean, not aware that special provisions and specific instructions have been made on her behalf. So she works away, unaware . . . oblivious to the plans of grace.

We, too, are most often incognizant of the gracious work of God behind the scenes. Every once in while we catch a hint of our Groomsman; most often, we work unmindful of His hand which is busy providing on our behalf.

GRACE DOESN'T ELIMINATE A RESPONSE OF DILIGENCE AND DISCIPLINE

God works in us to will and to *do* His good pleasure *(Philippians 2:13)*; God works everything out for us *(Romans 8:28)*, but God also works *with* us:

> And they went out and preached everywhere, while the Lord worked with them (Mark 16:20).

God works in us, for us, and with us.[5]

Recipients of grace are far from lazy:

> *So she gleaned in the field until evening. Then she beat out what she had gleaned, and it was about an ephah of barley. She took it up and went into the city* (Ruth 2:17–18a).

She didn't ask the servants to beat out the barley. She didn't ask anyone to carry what amounted to 25 pounds of grain back to the village, and she didn't even ask Boaz for a ride home.

There's a Latin proverb that says, "Providence assists not the idle."[6] That's another way of saying even God won't steer a parked car.

This is the principle of collaboration. Ruth went out to work and Boaz was working everything out.

In many ways, this illustrates the work of the Church—the Bride of Christ. We toil to advance the Gospel, and we work to make disciples.

J. Vernon McGee quipped in his little commentary on this text, "So many Christians sing at the top of their lungs, 'We shall come rejoicing, bringing in the sheaves,' and then go out and do nothing."[7]

An old Gospel song asks the penetrating question, "My house is full, but my field is empty; who will go and work for me today?" Even our Lord pointed out, *"The harvest is plentiful, but the workers are few"* (Matthew 9:37). The Gospel of grace is a collaborating effort between Christ and His Church.

Even though Ruth is in need of help from God, she is willing to work for God as He allows. And now, after a very long day, Ruth arrives home exhausted but satisfied.

Perhaps you're able to identify with her as you work hard in a volunteer or vocational ministry or maybe you are juggling the time demands of two jobs. You could be facing challenges on campus or in that corporate scene where you are striving for excellence in order to glorify Christ. You're undergoing strenuous tests of your faith, tirelessly raising a family to understand the Gospel, and you pillow your head at night, exhausted but satisfied.

Well, maybe just exhausted . . . and not so satisfied. There is still so much to do. Have you noticed that Christians you can count on to carry out some new responsibility are the people who already seem to have so much on their plate already?

Recipients of grace rarely take it for granted. And they're usually not napping. The Apostle Paul cheers us on: [Be] *not lagging behind in diligence; fervent in spirit, serving the Lord* (Romans 12:11). Someone put it like this,

"When I die, I want my body to leave skid marks." Frankly, grace often goes about its business in the lives of people who could actually use a nap.

We'll look at one more principle of grace, gleaned from the fields of Boaz.

GRACE AT WORK IN A PERSON'S LIFE SPILLS OVER INTO THE LIVES OF OTHERS

Ruth took up an ephah of barley (enough grain to live on for at least a month)

and went into the city, and her mother-in-law saw what she had gleaned. She also took it out and gave Naomi what she had left [a reference to her leftover meal from Boaz, which means Naomi can immediately eat a meal without having to cook anything]. *Her mother-in-law then said to her, "Where did you glean today and where did you work? May he who took notice of you be blessed"* (Ruth 2:18–19*a*).

Trust me, he will be!

So she told her mother-in-law with whom she had worked and said, "The name of the man with whom I worked today is Boaz." Naomi said to her daughter-in-law, "May he be blessed of the LORD who has not withdrawn his kindness to the living and to the dead." Again Naomi said to her, "The man is our relative, he is one of our closest relatives" [literally: he is a potential kinsman redeemer] (Ruth 2:19*b*–20).

One look at 25 pounds of barley and Naomi is hearing wedding bells. In fact, this is the first time we read of Naomi praising God.

The grace of God in Ruth's life has spilled over into Naomi's life. But don't misunderstand here: Naomi's joy is not based on Ruth, on Ruth's testimony, or on Ruth's experience . . . nor is our hope in anyone's experience or testimony.

The key thing to see here is that Naomi has hope in Boaz . . . who *he* is . . . what *he* said to Ruth . . . what *Boaz* can do for them both.

This is the lasting formula for Christian joy. We don't pin our hopes on anybody or anything other than Christ . . . what He has already done for us . . . what He has promised to do for us, His beloved, in the future.

The next day, Ruth will return to these fields of grace. She will glean there until ***the end of the barley harvest and the wheat harvest*** (Ruth 2:23), which would have been around seven weeks or so.

Did they enjoy lunch together again? We're not told, but you can easily imagine conversations and noontime luncheons, not to mention baskets of grain explained only in terms of grace:

- Grace takes the initiative and makes the first move.
- Grace surprises us with provision and protection.
- Grace plays the role of servant to those less worthy.
- Grace often works behind the scenes to provide for the beloved.
- Grace doesn't eliminate a response of diligence and discipline.
- Grace at work in a person's life spills over into the lives of others.

At the end of the harvest, Ruth and Boaz are deeply in love. Before we leave this scene, there are two more observations about grace.

GRACE DOESN'T DEAL SPORADICALLY IN YOUR LIFE—IT DEALS CONTINUOUSLY

Whether we notice it or not, grace is at work even now. We tend to notice the mountaintop experiences of God's grace at work. Take heart, He's working behind the scenes even as you trudge through that valley of difficulty or challenge.

Grace isn't fickle . . . your beloved Redeemer is committed for life.

YOU DON'T DRIFT IN AND OUT OF THE PRESENCE OF GRACE—YOU LIVE THERE

And God is able to make all grace abound to you, so that always having all sufficiency in everything, you may have an abundance for every good deed (2 Corinthians 9:8).

We are literally surrounded by grace. Oh, for eyes to see and hearts to sense and minds to appreciate the grace of God at work in our lives.

Ask your Redeemer to help you see and sense His love and provision for you—His Beloved—as you go through a new day with new pressures, new challenges, and new demands.

Ask Him for help, both to appreciate and understand that you, like Ruth, are literally working, serving, and living . . . in the fields of grace.

Then Naomi her mother-in-law said to her, "My daughter, shall I not seek security for you, that it may be well with you? ²*Now is not Boaz our kinsman, with whose maids you were? Behold, he winnows barley at the threshing floor tonight.* ³*Wash yourself therefore, and anoint yourself and put on your best clothes, and go down to the threshing floor; but do not make yourself known to the man until he has finished eating and drinking.* ⁴*It shall be when he lies down, that you shall notice the place where he lies, and you shall go and uncover his feet and lie down; then he will tell you what you shall do."* ⁵*She said to her, "All that you say I will do."*

⁶*So she went down to the threshing floor and did according to all that her mother-in-law had commanded her.* ⁷*When Boaz had eaten and drunk and his heart was merry, he went to lie down at the end of the heap of grain; and she came secretly, and uncovered his feet and lay down.* ⁸*It happened in the middle of the night that the man was startled and bent forward; and behold, a woman was lying at his feet.* ⁹*He said, "Who are you?" And she answered, "I am Ruth your maid. So spread your covering over your maid, for you are a close relative."* ¹⁰*Then he said, "May you be blessed of the LORD, my daughter. You have shown your last kindness to be better than the first by not going after young men, whether poor or rich."*

–Ruth 3:1–10

CHAPTER SIX

A MIDNIGHT PROPOSAL

Ruth 3:1–10

I t was Thanksgiving Day thirty-two years ago when I proposed marriage to my college sweetheart. It was the holiday break and a trip to her home for Thanksgiving was the perfect time to ask her parents' permission and, Lord willing, hear my blue-eyed beauty agree to marry me. I had the ring in my pocket.

I firmly believed in miracles.

In order to understand how I planned my proposal, let me give you a little background. I grew up in a home where there was an unwritten rule for all four Davey boys: "Don't bring a girl home from college unless you are engaged . . . or hope to be."

It was as simple as that. And none of us ever violated that principle. For the three years we had been dating while attending college in Tennessee, Marsha had never been to my home in Virginia. She knew why.

Of course, my parents had already met her and they agreed with me that she was a young lady of genuine character and, well, pretty to boot. So I had already received that all-important blessing from my folks.

I had the diamond engagement ring tucked away as we drove several hours to her childhood home in Atlanta.

I followed her father into the basement where he'd gone to fix the furnace. That was the only chance I'd had to get him alone. He was totally surprised by my request.

There's another story—behind the story—which you might appreciate. Since I had dated his daughter and had broken up with her in the past, he was actually planning to ask *me* a few questions over Thanksgiving break. He wanted to know what my intentions were toward his daughter. He figured I was going to keep beating around the bush. Instead, I beat him to the punch.

He said yes.

Later that day, when we were alone, I popped the question. "Marsha, I would really like to take you to my home this Christmas break." I paused to let that sink in. Her expression told me the implications were fairly obvious. I continued, "That is . . . if I can introduce you to everyone as my fiancée."

Another pause. Then the clincher, just in case it wasn't already perfectly clear: "That is . . . if you will marry me." She did a little bounce on her toes, wrung her hands, and said, "I don't know."

What?! That wasn't part of the plan. And that's certainly not how I imagined it.

If she were writing this story—I haven't agreed to co-authorship—she would tell you how, over the course of our dating history, I often did something significant to express my feelings—like write a love song or give her a promise ring—only to break up soon after.

It's called *cold feet*. And mine were terribly cold.

So when I proposed, her first thought was fear that if she said yes, I'd probably break up sometime in the near future.

For the next five minutes I gave her every good reason I could think of that I was serious and my mind was made up and, well, my feet had grown much warmer. After what seemed like an eternity, she finally said yes.

I've been telling people ever since that I definitely talked Marsha into marrying me.

Isn't it somewhat amazing to see the lengths to which young men will go to convince the love of their life to marry them?

Most men struggle with the same things: how to come up with the right timing, the right context, the right words, the right setting and, then, hopefully, receive the right *answer.*

Perhaps you've seen the online clip of a guy who proposed to his girlfriend during an NBA basketball game half-time. He'd worked out an elaborate plan, invited her to center court for reasons other than a proposal, and then as the cameras zoomed in and carried the scene to the jumbo screens and national television, he dropped to one knee and held out a ring. Her hands went to her mouth in shock. He said into his microphone, "Will you marry me?" Then the world held its breath and watched as she paused, shook her head no, and ran off the court in tears. Poor guy!

I did a little digging around on the subject of wedding proposals to see what kind of help there might be for guys—you know, those of us who need help coaxing their beloved into matrimony.

There's got to be a right way and a wrong way.

I came across one website promising information on "How to Propose Marriage." It started off by saying what *not* to do.

There were three no-nos:

1. Don't propose to your girlfriend in front of her parents.
   Okay, how obvious is that?
2. Don't put the ring in anything that is set in front of her to *eat*. The article warned, "The last thing you want to do is have to propose to her while she is being wheeled into surgery."
   Most guys would agree with that!
3. Don't propose marriage two days after meeting her.
   I found this especially insightful!

Do guys really need such basic advice? Don't answer that!

In my research, if you can call it that, I came across some marriage proposals that were stunning examples of how to do it the *wrong* way.

One lawyer made a deal with several policemen to arrest his girlfriend on totally bogus charges. They worked out the plan to stop her car, arrest her, and drive her to the city jail. Once incarcerated, they informed her that she could make one phone call. She called her lawyer boyfriend (of course); he came down and was taken to her cell, where he told her that the only way they would let her go was if she agreed to marry him.

How romantic.

Another was so shy he didn't quite know what to say when the moment arrived. He got all tongue-tied after he pulled out the ring box. He just froze. Then he tossed the box to his girlfriend and began to run away. She caught the box, saw what was inside, and had to chase him down to say yes.

Now *that's* cold feet.

Another young man pretended to have died. He'd planned the entire visitation at the funeral home with his buddies who worked there. He was all laid out in his best suit. His girlfriend stood by the casket, sobbing, when he suddenly sat up and asked her to marry him. After she finally stopped screaming, she slapped him . . . and then said yes.

They both need serious counseling.

But there were a couple of illustrations where the men got it right. And they pulled out all the stops.

One guy lived in a different state from his girlfriend and surprised her with a plane ticket to visit him. When she arrived, a limo was waiting for her, and the music playing over the car's system was actually a compilation of their favorite songs. She was taken to a high-end store where a rack of dresses and boxes of shoes were waiting for her, personally handpicked by him. She chose her favorites and was then driven to a salon for a three-hour treatment: massage, manicure, pedicure, hair styling, and makeup. Following that pampering pit stop, she was taken to a resort hotel, transferred to a horse-drawn carriage, and driven around a small lake to the entrance, where more than 100 candles lit the red carpet path. Violinists began to play a song this guy had actually composed, and as she walked the red carpet, he appeared at the top of the stairs and began to sing to her. When she stood on the top step, he dropped to one knee and a huge board behind him lit up with the words, "Will you marry me?" Before she could answer, he stood to his feet and sang the finale to his original love song, backed up by a 45-piece orchestra. When she said, "Yes," fireworks exploded in the sky above them.

This guy makes me sick! It's not fair to the rest of us who can hardly afford the ring *box*, much less fireworks. I hope my bride never reads this account because she just might ask, "And what were *you* thinking?"

There's one more proposal worth mentioning. A couple had bought an old repossessed home, understanding they were going to be married and this would be their first home. They didn't have much money and did all the repair work themselves. Since they spent so much time working on their little house, they had often walked the aisles of Home Depot together.

In fact, there were times when they were too tired to work, so they'd stroll around their local Home Depot and dream out loud of what they wanted to do next.

When the time for a marriage proposal came, the young man arranged it all . . . at Home Depot. He phoned his girlfriend and told her to meet him there that night. When she arrived at the store, the manager directed her to the Home and Garden section, where a table had been set with candlelight and a takeout dinner. He seated her, got down on one knee and proposed with a potted plant they could use in their new home. As she gushed out a yes, Home Depot employees nearby applauded.

Now that's my kind of proposal.

One of the most remarkable marriage proposals you will ever read about actually took place in this Old Testament love story. Only on *this* occasion it was the girl who did the proposing . . . and the planning. Ruth chose the right setting and just the right timing.

It would take place at midnight. But let's set the stage with a bit of the backstory:

> ***Ruth stayed close by the maids of Boaz in order to glean until the end of the barley harvest and the wheat harvest. And she lived with her mother-in-law*** (Ruth 2:23).

By now, Ruth and Boaz are definitely in love. Folks had stopped counting the lunch dates they'd enjoyed at the harvest field.

Boaz's field hands probably noticed that he'd never been more interested in these particular fields before.

But a problem is brewing.

When we arrive at chapter three, harvest time is over. Boaz and Ruth have actually parted, perhaps wondering if they will see each other again. Ruth has only recently settled back in with her mother-in-law, Naomi. But Naomi is not about to let grass grow under anybody's feet.

NAOMI'S RESOLVE

> ***Then Naomi her mother-in-law said to her, "My daughter, shall I not seek security for you that it may be well with you?"*** (Ruth 3:1).

That's a roundabout way of saying, "Ruth, we need to get you a husband." It was not unusual in those times for wedding plans to be worked out between the mother and daughter in what was referred to as simply "the mother's chamber." Since Naomi was more like a mother to Ruth, she takes on that matchmaking responsibility.

I can imagine Naomi sitting Ruth down and saying something like, "Ruth, I'm not going to be around forever to help you through life in this strange new land you've chosen for your own. It's obvious that Boaz is interested in you—he's been dumping grain in your path for weeks now; he's invited you to lunch time and again, and he's even had his staff bring you water whenever you want it. He's obviously in love with you."

Naomi removes any doubt from the reader's mind when Samuel records her asking Ruth a rhetorical question, ***"Is not Boaz our kinsman?"*** (Ruth 3:2*a*).

According to Old Testament law, a widow could actually demand that the next closest relative who was willing and available would marry her.[1] It was God's plan for a marriage to provide her with financial security. Furthermore, any children born to them would be given the name of her *first* husband. That would secure his name for another generation and his family farm or estate would remain in his particular family *(Deuteronomy 25:5–10)*.

So, according to this provision, Ruth was actually free to take the initiative. Her condition was not the same as that of an unmarried woman. In that case, the man was to take the initiative. As a widow, it was her right to let her intentions be known to the kinsman. It was her move.[2]

Naomi urges, "Ruth, harvest season is over . . . you may never have another chance like this . . . you might not even see Boaz until next year. He can redeem you if he wants. It's time to let him know you want him to become your husband."

Ruth is obviously a stranger to these customs. She's a Moabitess, not a Jew. These laws were still foreign to her and she probably asked Naomi, "Well, then, what do you want me to do?"

Naomi, the matchmaker says, "I'm glad you asked!"

"Behold, he winnows barley at the threshing floor tonight"
(Ruth 3:2*b*).

How did she know that?! Well, she just knows. She's been planning this proposal for weeks. She knows that Boaz and his crew are threshing that very night.

Now, I was raised in the city. My father was raised on a farm—in fact, he can talk about planting and baling and threshing. Had he not been led by God into the ministry before getting married, I would have grown up on a farm in Minnesota . . . milking cows at four o'clock in the morning.

I asked my Dad a couple of months ago, "How did you and your siblings endure sub-zero weather in a barn, milking cows in the dead of winter?" He said, "Well, your hands stayed warm as you milked the cows there in the barn, but you also made sure you sat real *close* to the cow." I'm so glad that God called my father into the ministry!

Growing up, we'd travel to Minnesota each summer for a family reunion. And, among other events, we'd drive out to attend the Threshing Bee there in the small farming community of Butterfield. It seemed like the entire town of 900 would show up. All the farmers would bring out their threshing equipment from generations past and display it. A few farmers would even operate some of their old threshing machinery out in the field.

These were some of the most boring days of my life—the Threshing Bee in Butterfield. But not for those farmers and my aunts, uncles, and parents. They *loved* it. The reasons weren't as obvious to my young mind as they are now. That machinery had changed *everything* for their families, many of whom had been farming for generations.

The Threshing Bee was nothing less than a thanksgiving celebration for the creativity and ingenuity of inventive minds. The development of threshing machinery had helped them provide for their families . . . and their nation.

Threshing floors in Old Testament times were constructed out in the open fields. They were nothing more than a patch of ground, usually selected at a high spot on a ridge where they could catch the night breeze.[3]

A large, flat open area was raked off and swept clean to the ground, then sprinkled lightly with water. Rocks were piled around the perimeter, creating a round, smooth area—a threshing floor.

The sheaves of grain were brought in on the backs of the workers, donkeys, camels, oxen, or whatever the owner could use to carry them. They were heaped in the circular threshing floor, then two or three animals were harnessed shoulder-to-shoulder and simply driven around and around the floor as their hooves separated the husks from the kernels. Then winnowers took a shovel or pitchfork and tossed the sheaves into the air, allowing the breeze to carry the chaff/empty husks away while the heavier grain fell to the threshing floor.[4, 5]

The men, women, and children worked late into the night. It was always a time of celebration simply because the harvest was being brought in. And remember, **Ruth 1:1** informs us that the land of Israel had experienced a terrible famine. By comparing other passages, we know that this famine lasted seven years. Later in **Ruth 1:6**, Naomi returned to Bethlehem because she'd heard that there was no longer a famine.

We have every reason to believe that this is the *first* crop Israel has experienced in seven years. Good times had returned to Bethlehem. Although threshing was a time of hard work, the mood was one of laughter and joy and feasting. Godly Israelites like Boaz would have been celebrating the goodness of God.

We also know from other passages of Scripture that during these days of the judges, Midianites had made a habit of invading the land and stealing the crops that had been threshed.[6] Boaz is here at this scene, no doubt, to help protect his bumper crop from theft.

All of this sets the stage for Ruth's proposal . . . this is her last chance before Boaz will leave the fields for many months. If there ever was a perfect time to make her desires known to Boaz, this would have been her last—and best—opportunity.

There are a few more details in Naomi's plan. She tells Ruth, **"Wash yourself"** (Ruth 3:3a). This Hebrew verb signifies the full treatment. She got a manicure and pedicure, and the Mary Kay lady came out to the house to make sure Ruth's makeup and clothing were done according to her color chart.

Next, Naomi commanded, **"[A]noint yourself"** [literally: put on perfume] (Ruth 3:3a). There was plenty to choose from, even among the poorest of people. Fifteen hundred years before the birth of Christ, the queen of Egypt was sending scouting parties all around the known world to bring her the latest perfumes for her collection.

Ruth must have kept a bottle or two from her old life back home. J. Vernon McGee used to say that her favorite perfume was probably called "Midnight in Moab."

Naomi then said, **"[P]ut on your best clothes"** (Ruth 3:3a). In other words, "Get all dolled up . . . it might be dark out there, but you never know, Boaz might call for a lantern."

Naomi has even thought through the timing issue. In the latter part of this verse, she carefully instructs Ruth:

"**[G]***o down to the threshing floor; but do not make yourself known to the man until he has finished eating and drinking*** (Ruth 3:3*b*).

What a wise woman. Wait until the man's had his dinner before you try something major. That's timeless advice, isn't it? Before you show your husband the dent in the car, Junior's report card, or ask him to paint the house a different color, feed him.

Naomi says even further for Ruth to wait until they lie down to sleep. She doesn't want to interrupt Boaz while he's working on his ledger.

There's a strange detail that's worth a closer look:

"**[Y]***ou shall notice the place where he lies, and you shall go and uncover his feet and lie down; then he will tell you what you shall do*" (Ruth 3:4).

Some would suggest that Ruth is told to go down and proposition him sexually; that *uncovering his feet* must be some sort of euphemism for sexual relations.

Nothing could be further from the truth.

We already know by now that Boaz is a godly man. And in a few verses he will praise Ruth for her *moral character*—hardly fitting if she's just asked him to violate God's moral standard.

Boaz will refuse to touch Ruth until he has the legal right of kinsman redeemer. In fact, he asks her to leave the threshing floor before the break of dawn so that both of their reputations can be above suspicion.

We also learn from the Mishna, a commentary on Jewish customs and laws, that a man was forbidden to act as kinsman redeemer toward a Gentile woman he had already been sexually involved with outside of marriage.[7] This would obviously protect a vulnerable widow from being abused or taken advantage of by a man who should have redeemed her *first*. And according to Jewish custom and law, if a potential kinsman redeemer didn't redeem the widow, he also forfeited the right to her former husband's property.

All that to say, he's gotta marry her first!

Like the old rhyme:

> *First comes love,*
> *Then comes marriage,*
> *Then comes baby in the baby carriage.*

That's pretty good theology. And it also happens to remain the progression God designed to protect both women *and* men.

Ruth is not making some kind of lurid proposition to Boaz. She is told by Naomi to go down where he's sleeping and uncover his feet. There's no secret meaning to that phrase. Ruth was to literally take the blanket off his feet, which would cause Boaz to wake up—slowly—without startling him.

> *So she went down to the threshing floor, and did according to all that her mother-in-law had commanded her. When Boaz had eaten and drunk and his heart was merry, he went to lie down at the end of the heap of grain* (Ruth 3:6–7a).

Still others suggest that Boaz was drunk and Ruth took advantage of his incoherent state and talked him into marrying her. Again, the text answers such sordid commentary which evidently can't stand the sight of a godly man or woman bonding their hearts in purity and love. The text says he had eaten and drunk and his ***heart was merry***.

The Hebrew idiom *yatab leb* simply means he was "in good spirits."[8] We would say that he was in a great mood.

And why not! This is a bumper crop. The famine is over. There's a huge pile of grain on the threshing floor. Is this a perfect night, or what?

RUTH'S REQUEST

Now notice ***it happened in the middle of the night*** (Ruth 3:8a). The Hebrew text literally reads "in the half of the night," which means it was midnight.[9] So Boaz was awakened as he realized his feet were cold, and as he bent forward to cover them, he was startled to see the form of a woman lying at his feet.

The word translated *startled* can also be translated better, I believe, *shivered*.[10] You can almost see the scene unfolding. Boaz's uncovered feet are cold. He wakes up shivering, sits up, and bends forward to put the blanket back over his feet . . . and discovers he's not alone:

> *He said "Who are you?" And she answered, "I am Ruth your maid. So spread your covering over your maid, for you are a close relative"* [literally: you are a redeemer] (Ruth 3:9).

This is tantamount to the widow Ruth asking Boaz, "Will you marry me?"

Can you imagine? Boaz is in his pajamas . . . he's been snoring away; his hair is all messed up. . . is this love, or what?

He wakes up to cover his feet and there's the woman he's fallen in love with. She leans toward his stubbled face and whispers, "Boaz, I'm here to remind you that you have a legal right to marry me—will you accept that right and make me your wife?"

Before we note Boaz's answer, we need to understand why all the secrecy. Why has Ruth come at midnight with her proposal?

It's likely that she has come out of respect for his character, not wanting to demand her rights publically—not wanting to force him to have to make a decision before the elders at the city gate.

I believe it's even more likely that Naomi and Ruth already know there is another man first in line (as we'll discover later) with the first right of refusal to the hand of Ruth.

Ruth has come secretly to let Boaz know her heart's desire is for *him* to redeem her rather than the other potential suitor. She has slipped into the field to let him know that her heart belongs to him.

Take a look at how carefully she's worded her proposal with two significant word choices.

A Symbolic Custom

Ruth asked Boaz to **spread your covering over your maid** (Ruth 3:9). She's not asking for his blanket because it's cold out there; she's referring to the Jewish custom of the bridegroom placing a talith upon his bride on their wedding day. A talith was a fringed garment belonging to him that now covers her, signifying that he will take on the responsibilities of care and authority.[11]

Ruth is effectively saying, "Will you cover me with your care and authority?" In simpler terms, "Will you marry me?"

A Significant Word

Ruth not only refers to a symbolic custom, she uses a significant word in her proposal—a derivative of the word Boaz used when they first met, when he said to her,

> **"May the LORD reward your work and your wages be full from the LORD, the God of Israel, under whose wings you have come to seek refuge"** (Ruth 2:12).

That word translated *wings* is the same word Ruth now uses as she asked Boaz to spread his *covering*—his *wings*—over her. Ruth is actually asking Boaz to become the answer to his own prayer.[12]

She is asking Boaz to *become* the application of his own intercession. Ruth was whispering to Boaz there on the threshing floor at midnight, "Do you remember that prayer you made on my behalf a few months ago? Would you like to be the answer to your own prayer and become the wings under which I find refuge?"

BOAZ'S RESPONSE

Now the question remains: Will Boaz's feet stay cold?

Not in a million years.

He can hardly contain himself. Boaz whispers back, ***"May you be blessed of the LORD, my daughter"*** (Ruth 3:10).

In the Hebrew manuscripts, that's one word: "Yeehaw!"

Actually, Boaz's immediate praise is to God for this remarkable woman. His willing answer is yes! He will give a longer answer, as well as raise a serious problem with her proposal.

But that's for our next chapter.

¹⁰ Then he said, "May you be blessed of the LORD, my daughter. You have shown your last kindness to be better than the first by not going after young men, whether poor or rich. ¹¹ Now, my daughter, do not fear. I will do for you whatever you ask, for all my people in the city know that you are a woman of excellence. ¹² Now it is true I am a close relative; however, there is a relative closer than I. ¹³ Remain this night, and when morning comes, if he will redeem you, good; let him redeem you. But if he does not wish to redeem you, then I will redeem you, as the LORD lives. Lie down until morning."

¹⁴ So she lay at his feet until morning and rose before one could recognize another; and he said, "Let it not be known that the woman came to the threshing floor." ¹⁵ Again he said, "Give me the cloak that is on you and hold it." So she held it, and he measured six measures of barley and laid it on her. Then she went into the city. ¹⁶ When she came to her mother-in-law, she said, "How did it go, my daughter?" And she told her all that the man had done for her. ¹⁷ She said, "These six measures of barley he gave to me, for he said, 'Do not go to your mother-in-law empty-handed.'"

–Ruth 3:10–17

SEVEN REASONS TO SAY, "I DO"

Ruth 3:10–17

In an email I received with a number of interesting facts highlighting our ever-changing culture, one stood out: more than twenty-five percent of American couples who married met *online.*

One researcher of this subject recorded that conservative estimates indicate there are currently 50 million people who are using online dating services.[1]

I am pastor to a number of wonderful couples in our church who met through some kind of online dating service. One of them recently came up to me and laughed about their earlier "compatibility tests" online and said, "Now that we're married, we've realized how entirely different we are from each other."

Which is a good thing, right? I mean, who really wants to marry someone just like themselves? How weird would that be? Besides, if you marry someone who thinks exactly like you do, one of you is unnecessary!

Frankly, there aren't any Bible verses on how to find your mate or how to communicate with someone in order to biblically fall in love.

Fortunately, by the time I started dating, the telephone had been invented—you remember: that black glossy plastic thing that used to hang on the wall of your kitchen.

However, there needs to be a warning issued. In fact, the troubling thing to me is that the leading principle—the key word, if you will, promised by online dating services—that has everyone's attention and is pursued by millions of people world-wide is the word *compatibility.*

One dating service website promises to match you with numerous dimensions of compatibility which are "scientifically based predictors of long-term relationship success."[2]

That promise sounds like trouble, to me: *scientifically based predictors of long-term relationship success.*

Reports are now estimating that as many as ninety percent of online daters are lying about something related to the *real* them.

One researcher wrote, "For men, the major areas of deception in an online relationship are their income and marital status; for women, the major areas of lying are their physical attributes and their age."[3]

So—an online service that promises to provide you with scientifically based predictors for relationship success may actually be matching you with someone who isn't exactly the person they are self-describing!

Online dating services are now estimating—and I'm telling you this to further terrify you—that at least twelve percent of online male suitors are, indeed, *married.*

An even more common problem is that singles are developing online relationships with *more* than one person at a time.

I'll never forget watching a documentary where both a husband and wife were cheating with someone they met through an online dating service for local singles. After weeks of online dating, they decided they were perfect for each other and agreed to finally meet at a local restaurant. When they arrived, this husband and wife discovered that they were having dinner with each other!

Evidently, they had been exactly what they were looking for all along.

One of my pastoral associates who works with older singles told me of several individuals in our fellowship who were stung by this very issue. One woman discovered the man she was falling in love with online was involved with another woman online at the same time.

Another couple developed a dating relationship, then canceled their wedding plans because they soon discovered that what had matched them online didn't translate into real life.

My associate has encouraged our singles that online dating sites should only be used to provide an *introduction*. He advises them to spend no less than six months of dating that individual in person, where they can be observed making decisions, relating to others, choosing friends and, most importantly, relating to the body of Christ.

That's great advice.

Whether dating online or live, we all know the temptation of wanting to put our best foot forward, right? Everyone does that . . . hopefully in an honest manner.

On my first date with the girl who would become my wife, I walked to her dormitory to pick her up and take her to a church service. And did I ever put my best foot forward. I showed up wearing my best suit: it was navy blue, thick wool with wide mafia-style pinstripes—never mind that it was 95 degrees outside . . . this was my best suit! I also had on my favorite dark blue dress shirt and a solid white tie made of 100% polyester (think glow-in-the-dark). And to top it off, I was wearing baby blue saddle oxfords.

When she opened the door to greet me, she nearly fainted. I assumed she was quite impressed.

Much later . . . *much* later . . . she told me what she *really* thought about my appearance. She remembered, "I really wanted to *be* with you; I just didn't want to be *seen* with you."

It probably would have gone better if I'd met her online!

Let's be honest. We all are fallen creatures. Romance in real life is actually between two sinners.[4]

And don't get me wrong; similar tastes and desires and interests are wonderful things, but the differences and distinctives and perspectives in your God-created spouse are intended to complement and broaden and develop and deepen who you are and how you think and, ultimately, how you live.

Think about that for a moment: *we* are the Bride of Christ. How compatible are we with Him?!

The search for Mister or Miss Right is not a search for someone like *you*—it should be a search for someone who wants to be like *Christ*.

Consider the fact that a biblical view of marriage is not so much about compatibility as it is about *character* . . . and complementing one another. Which means there are differences God actually built into us that need to be ironed out; He put us together so we could develop sharpened perspectives and thought processes and balanced, biblical thinking.

Two fallen sinners, seeking God's grace and His will for their lives, end up covenanting to love each other for better or for worse. That's the greatest illustration on earth of the love of Christ for the Church *(Ephesians 5:32)*.

So the starting place is *conversion*—whether that person knows, loves, and trusts Jesus Christ in a living, genuine, demonstrable manner. Ask yourself if their Christianity is a secret. If it is, your relationship will sour. In fact, if they don't honor Christ, you may very well be treated dishonorably yourself.

The next major step beyond conversion is *character*. That will make all the difference in the world. Character goes way beyond personal tastes, sports interests, and music preferences. Character forms the foundation upon which a godly relationship is built.

So . . . how do you detect character?

If Boaz and Ruth each had a checklist for a spouse, what would have been on *their* list?

And by the way, *no one* would have ever matched them . . . talk about incompatible!

They were totally different in just about every way, beginning with family backgrounds, traditions, and demographics:

- one had grown up in idolatry and pagan religion, the other had grown up a follower of God;

- one was rich, the other was poor;

- one was a business owner, the other a migrant worker;

- one was single, the other had been married;

- one had experienced the death of a spouse, the other hadn't;

- one was a mature believer, the other a new believer;

- one was financially independent; the other lived hand-to-mouth.

The list could go on and on.

But they had this in common: commitment to the God of Abraham, Isaac, and Jacob and genuine character in following His leadership.

In fact, from their love story and, especially, their brief encounter at the threshing floor, we can easily make several observations about genuine character.

These observations ought to be the checklist for every single individual who is praying for a mate. They also serve as a wonderful set of goals for every married person to pursue on a daily basis. This list is not for someone else to match as much as it is for us to mirror.

The scene at the threshing floor provides seven character qualities in the life of Boaz and Ruth.

SPIRITUALITY

The relationship between Boaz and God was no secret; it was daily and alive. In the days of the judges when everybody did that which was right in their own eyes, Boaz lived with a sense of spiritual awareness.

When we first met him in chapter two, he asked for God's blessing on his employees. When he met Ruth, he prayed that God would shelter her under His wings.

And now at the threshing floor, after the love of his life asks him to become her kinsman redeemer—to marry her and buy up her late husband's estate and pay off all her family's debts—the first thing Boaz says is ***"May you be blessed of the LORD, my daughter"*** (Ruth 3:9)—"God bless you, Ruth."

This wasn't an act or a put-on. This was reality. Boaz had a vital, active, living, walking, breathing relationship with God. This is foundational. This is where you begin. We read this verse before:

> *Unless the LORD builds the house, they labor in vain who build it* (Psalm 127:1).

This is why, when performing a wedding ceremony, I ask the bride and groom before the vows are exchanged, "Can you say in the presence of these witnesses that you have accepted Jesus Christ into your life as Lord and Savior?"

For those of you who are single, it really won't take very long for you to discover whether that person is sincerely walking with Christ:

- Do they talk about Him?
- Do they want to please Him?

- Do they live for Him?

- Do they encourage you to follow Him?

- Have you ever seen their Bible?

- Have you ever seen them reading their Bible?

- Do they love the Church?

- Are they involved in service for Christ?

- Do they want others to hear the Gospel?

Listen, a genuine spiritual desire for God and the things of God is more than attending church with you on Sunday. If that's all you ever know of their spiritual side, I highly recommend that you stop seeing them.

HUMILITY

Humility is another character quality I observe in Boaz. Spirituality and humility don't necessarily show up in the same body, but when Boaz responded to Ruth's proposal by saying, ***"You have shown your last kindness to be better than the first by not going after young men, whether poor or rich"*** (Ruth 3:10), he was effectively saying, "I can't believe you chose *me*."

The reference by Boaz to Ruth's first kindness is probably a reference to Ruth's care for Naomi.[5] But he then adds that *this* act of kindness—wanting to marry him—is more amazing than choosing to care for Naomi. In other words, Boaz responds with, "Ruth, you are so *kind* to want to marry *me*."

Keep in mind that we are told nothing of Boaz's age, although his reference to her as his daughter indicates he might be older. Further, the Bible doesn't tell us anything about his looks or his physique.[6]

We don't know if he was tall, dark, and handsome or tall, skinny, and bald—which is *so* much better looking, from my wife's perspective!

What we do know is that Boaz was wealthy enough to own fertile fields and to hire employees.

So get this picture in your mind: here's a destitute widow from a foreign country, one step away from being a beggar, with nothing tangible to offer but debt and potential scorn . . . and Boaz says, "I am so thrilled you want me."

His humility is staggering.

In his culture he was at the top of the food chain. He had many more reasons to be proud than humble. He had every reason to tell Ruth, "Are you kidding . . . you want *me* to marry *you?*"

But if you've been reading closely, just about every time he opens his mouth, the quality of humility comes out. He doesn't look down on her at all. In fact, we'll discover that he's well aware of her character and commitment to God . . . and as far as he's concerned, that erases all those other incompatibilities.

PRIORITY

You might want to add to your list another character quality: priority. Boaz knows what matters most. And so does Ruth, evidently. He goes on to say, "Listen, the reason I'm so pleased with your proposal and I want to say yes is because ***all my people in the city know that you are a woman of excellence***" (Ruth 3:11*b*).

Boaz doesn't say:

- because you are a woman of great beauty;
- because you are a woman of rare talent and personality;
- because you are a woman of high fashion;
- because you are a woman who likes softball and strawberry ice cream, just like me.

No . . . he actually says that she is a woman of noble character. This same word is translated *virtuous* in *Proverbs 31*. This Hebrew adjective refers to a person of moral strength.

Boaz and Ruth were seemingly incompatible in just about every conceivable way *except* character.

HONESTY

A fourth checkpoint in this godly list is the word honesty. There on the threshing floor everything is going so well. Boaz and Ruth are obviously in love with one another. This couldn't be more perfect.

But then Boaz drops a nuclear bomb, shattering the mood and the moment. He adds, ***"Now, it is true I am a close relative; however, there is*** *a relative closer than I"* (Ruth 3:12). This is the law of the *goel*—the kins-man redeemer.

There is deep anguish in this admission. Boaz effectively tells Ruth that he *can't* redeem her because another man is a closer relative to her father-in-law than he is. And that other relative has the right to marry Ruth.

Well, I can imagine Ruth beginning to cry. Had Naomi told her? Did Ruth already know and go to the threshing floor anyway to inform Boaz that she really wanted *him* to redeem her instead?

We don't know.

What we do know is that after Boaz tells her that he loves her and would be thrilled to marry her, he tells her the truth—even if it ruined the party.

He basically says to her, "Listen, Ruth, I would love to redeem you as your closest relative, but I'm not the guy . . . there's someone older than I am and, thus, first in line for the right to redeem you."

Now in today's culture, Boaz would have gotten a lawyer to sue the other guy for his rights or hired a hit man to bump the guy off. He would have found a counselor to tell him to follow his heart and do whatever made him happy. He might have even found a spiritual leader to tell him the law of a kinsman redeemer was for a different context and culture and, besides, they were centuries old and no longer relevant.

He could have easily talked to friends who would certainly encourage him, saying, "Look Boaz, you're not getting any younger; you love her and she loves you and these are the days of the judges where everybody does what is right in their own eyes—and if it's right for you, man, then it's all right . . . get over your Victorian guilt and go for it."

Any of that sound familiar?

Instead, Boaz simply says, "Ruth, I've gotta be honest and tell you there's somebody closer in line than me."

Spirituality, humility, priority, honesty . . . and that's not all.

ACCOUNTABILITY

Now, as I read and reread this text, I found it hard to imagine any man in Boaz's sandals saying these next words:

"Remain this night; and when morning comes, if he will redeem you, good; let him redeem you. But if he does not

***wish to redeem you, then I will redeem you, as the LORD
lives"*** (Ruth 3:13).

Did we read that right? ***If he will redeem you,*** **good; *let him redeem
you.*** Are you kidding me? Is Boaz some kind of concrete block with no feelings? Is his heart made out of cement? "Look Ruth, if that other guy wants
to marry you, that's fine and dandy with me!"

Not on your life . . . we've already read his first response. Boaz is a man
of character, to the point where he submits his emotions to the Word of God.

This matter must be settled legally.[7]

Find someone and *become* someone who is willing to set aside personal
feelings in order to do what is right and you're well on your way to finding
and becoming a man or woman worthy of saying, "I do."

And if you're on the hunt, ask yourself this question: does that other
person I'm falling in love with submit their emotions and their passions and
their feelings to the Word of God? Do they do the right thing, no matter
how they feel?

This is illustrated so well by that little seven-year-old girl who obviously
had her emotions under control, much like Boaz here. Evidently, an eight-
year-old boy in her Sunday school class asked her to marry him. She was
overheard saying, "I *can't* marry you." He protested, "Why not?" She said,
"Well, my daddy married my mommy, my grandpa married my grandma,
and all my uncles married my aunts, so we can't get married, because we're
not related."[8]

I love that . . . we gotta do what's right.

And here's something easy to overlook: Boaz was willing to remain single
and lose the love of his life rather than disobey the Word of God.

Frankly, he had already thought it through. But instead of coming up
with loopholes in the covenant of God, he would begin to strategize on how
to approach the other redeemer who was closer in line to Ruth. Boaz would
settle for nothing less than concluding the matter according to the laws of
God.

Let me put this in practical terms: if that individual you're interested in
does not honor the Word of God, you have no assurance they will live an
honorable life.

PURITY

There's another word that surfaces at midnight in Bethlehem: purity. Boaz said, *"Lie down until morning"* (Ruth 3:13c). And just where did Ruth lie down? *So she lay at his feet until morning* (Ruth 3:14a).

There's little doubt that Boaz could have taken advantage of this situation. They are both deeply in love with each other; they are committed to finding a way to get married; Ruth is clearly vulnerable as a widow. She's expressed her love to him and he, to her . . . what more do they need?

But there was no advantage taken that night; no solicitation offered; no dismissal of moral standards. This midnight dialogue became an amazing demonstration of purity.

What you have here in Bethlehem this night are two sinners highly committed to God. Two people quietly pledging their love, choosing to wait in purity to see what God will do.

GENEROSITY

One final observation of character is often overlooked in our haste to the next scene. It's a word that needs fleshing out in godly men and women.

Boaz fills Ruth's bag with barley and tells her to take it home *(Ruth 3:15)*. His specific command retold by Ruth to Naomi was, *"Do not go to your mother-in-law empty handed"* (Ruth 3:17).

Why would he bother? At this point, Boaz has every reason to keep his money and his grain. However, he remains sensitive to the needs of these two widows. Bible scholars estimate that the amount of grain given will sustain Ruth and Naomi for at least two weeks.

This lets us know that Boaz is no doubt thinking that within two weeks the matter will be resolved and these women will be cared for permanently as members of his household—at least, that's what he's hoping will happen.

May I predict for you that if that person you're interested in is stingy and selfish, you should not anticipate generosity to follow the wedding ceremony. Watch how they use their money. Do they hoard what they have? Do they spend money only on themselves? Do they give money to ministry? Do they tip well and care for the financial needs of their parents? Are they cheap?

Here in Bethlehem is a man showing genuine care and rare generosity. James the Apostle calls it *pure* religion, caring for widows in their need *(James 1:27)*.

So that's the checklist from the romance novel of Boaz and Ruth. And remember, it isn't as much about compatibility as it is about character.

You should never stop pursuing these attributes of character, no matter how old you are. Frankly, you have no idea what a person can become when applying these characteristics to his or her life. And that goes for you and me.

Yes, these are the attributes to pray for in someone else. These are the ones we should seek to foster in the life of our spouse. At the same time, these observations of genuine character must be pursued by each of us . . . at all costs . . . without letting up . . . for the rest of our lives.

This is the kind of person to *find* . . . this is the kind of person to *become* . . . this is the kind of person to *keep*.

Then she said, "Wait, my daughter, until you know how the matter turns out; for the man will not rest until he has settled it today."

–Ruth 3:18

CHAPTER EIGHT

THE LONGEST DAY

Ruth 3:18

A news report delivered the story of how unmet desires escalated into emergency calls. Evidently, a twenty-seven-year-old woman in Fort Pierce, Florida, walked into a McDonald's to get a 10-piece McNuggets meal. After standing in line for some time, she finally made it to the counter and ordered her dinner. The employee took her order and her money, only to return moments later to inform the customer that they had just run out of McNuggets: those low-sodium, fat-free delights . . . *okay, I added that description.*

When told that she could choose something else from the menu, the customer refused and demanded, "Just give me my money back." The employee apologized and told her that all sales were final. He did remind her that she could get something else from the menu—even if it cost more—at no extra charge. "No way," this woman insisted, "it's McNuggets or my money back." She couldn't be coaxed into eating a Big Mac, a McRib, or even a Quarter Pounder with cheese and jumbo fries.

She became so angry that she stood at the counter and dialed 911—three times.

I mean, is this an emergency, or what?

She never got her McNuggets . . . but when the police arrived, she did get a ticket for misusing the 911 emergency system.[1]

I couldn't help wondering how many of us treat God like He's an employee at McDonald's. We want something for ourselves and we've even paid a fair price in order to get it. God doesn't deliver, and we're left at the counter with options we never wanted. Even worse, we wait at the counter while God seems to disappear with our money; we're left waiting for Him to return and offer some guidance, or guarantee . . . some indication of what to do next.

When God finally does appear, He demands that we partake of something we don't like . . . something we would never have ordered in the first place.

One of the greatest tests of a Christian's faith is standing at a vacant counter, waiting patiently on the sovereign direction of God. An even greater test of our faith is when God reappears to hand us something we never would have chosen.

We can identify with Margaret Thatcher, former prime minister of England, who once said, "I am extremely patient, provided I get my own way in the end."[2]

That's not really patience. If it were, we would all be perfectly patient as we stood at empty counters, expecting to receive whatever it was we wanted.

In that convicting little book of Puritan prayers *The Valley of Vision*, one church leader of generations ago admitted in prayer his personal struggle with patient surrender:

> *When Thou wouldst guide me, I control myself.*
> *When Thou wouldst be sovereign, I rule myself.*
> *When I should depend on Thy provision, I supply myself.*
> *When I should submit to Thy providence, I follow my own will.*
> *When I should honor and trust Thee, I serve myself.*
> *Lord, it is my chief desire to bring my heart back to Thee.*[3]

This is the honest confession of a heart that admits how hard it is to wait; how difficult it is to surrender without any guarantee from God.

Without a doubt, the longest day in the life of Ruth is about to begin. It will be a day that requires patient surrender. And she holds no guarantee from God that Boaz will become her redeemer.

According to Old Testament law, Ruth's kinsman redeemer would buy up the family estate of Elimelech and take her and Naomi into his care. There was just that one little catch to the deal: another man is more closely related to Naomi's family, and he has first dibs on the land that belonged to

Naomi's late husband. Jewish tradition taught that this man was a brother to the late Elimelech.

And he has first dibs on *Ruth*.

This isn't just about love . . . it involves the Law.

Both Boaz and Ruth, in a remarkable demonstration of character and honesty, have revealed that they are willing to submit to the Law of God as revealed through Moses.

BOAZ'S PROMISE

The one promise Ruth presently clings to is her beloved assuring her that he will do everything in his power to settle the matter of her redemption as soon as possible:

> ***"Remain this night, and when morning comes, if he*** [this other relative] ***will redeem you, good; let him redeem you. But, if he does not wish to redeem you, then I will redeem you, as the LORD lives"*** (Ruth 3:13).

I love that brief comment that reveals the passion and emotion in the heart of Boaz: ***"I will redeem you, as the LORD lives!"***—literally: *by the life of Yahweh.*

He is making an oath, a vow, to Ruth: he will redeem her at all possible costs, and she can believe his promise with the same assurance that she can believe in the existence of Yahweh.[4]

It's not unusual to fasten a little addendum to our promises; it gives them an even greater sense of importance or gravity. Kids say things like, "Cross my heart, hope to die, stick a needle in my eye." That's about the worst thing a kid can imagine. Actually, I'm still there—getting stuck with a needle *anywhere* would add gravity to a promise from me!

People also say, "I swear on a stack of Bibles" or "I promise you on my mother's grave."

Here's Boaz claiming the *ultimate* foundation for his oath: "As God is alive, I am making you this promise." In other words, "Ruth, if that other relative doesn't want you, as God is our true and living God, I will redeem you."

Boaz not only makes a promise, he makes *provision* for her as he gives her enough grain the next morning to meet Naomi's and her needs for at least two more weeks.

Perhaps Boaz was thinking this relative might be away or at his own threshing site, and Boaz doesn't want Ruth to have to go out and forage for grain and risk being put in harm's way. So, again, he loads her down with grain.

Early the next morning, Ruth heads for home and Boaz goes to the city gates, where a plan he's begun formulating will soon play out.

NAOMI'S QUESTION

As soon as Ruth walks through the front door, Naomi asked, ***"How did it go, my daughter?"*** (Ruth 3:16*a*). Translated literally, the Hebrew reads, "Who are you?" . . . which seems really strange, doesn't it? Did Naomi not recognize Ruth in the early morning light?

The Hebrew language clarifies this, as the expression carries the idea of, "Who are you *now?*" So Naomi's question really means, "Now that you've met Boaz at the threshing floor and told him your desire, are you *now* the future bride of Boaz, or what? In what state are you now?"

Bible scholars have attempted to translate this question in order to convey the best sense of the Hebrew language. My translation reads, "How did it go?" Others translate it, "How art thou?" or "How did you fare?".

Naomi is basically asking, "Did he say yes?!" She's already picked out the wedding dress, the bridal bouquet, and . . . what's that mouth-watering aroma? Do we smell wedding cake already baking in the oven?

> ***And she*** [Ruth] ***told her all that the man had done for her***
> (Ruth 3:16*b*).

Ruth explained everything that Boaz had promised and the vow that he had made to her. You can see and hear them excitedly going over every word and examining every expression on Boaz's face . . . every nuance of tone and attitude.

And there was no doubt about it: Boaz wanted to marry her.

NAOMI'S COUNSEL

Then Naomi said to her,

> ***"Wait, my daughter, until you know how the matter turns out; for the man will not rest until he has settled it today"***
> (Ruth 3:18).

"Wait, my daughter" can be translated "Sit still."

Are you kidding? *Sit still?* That's right. This is about to become the longest day in Ruth's life.[5] And Naomi's, too, by the way.

They probably drove each other nuts all day long, peeking out the window . . . jumping up at the sound of every passing cart . . . looking out the door for any sign of a messenger or relative to deliver the news . . . watching the sundial in the courtyard.

Sit still? Hardly.

There's rich truth in that command. There really isn't anything Ruth *can* do. She is powerless to redeem herself. The law can only reveal to her the condition she is in and the total dependency she must have upon her redeemer.[6]

What a wonderful picture of the believer, the Bride of Christ. Like Ruth, all that we ever do is tell Christ we love Him and want to be taken under His authority and care; we want to rest under His wings. And when we do, we discover that Christ loved us first and He is at work on our behalf.

Christ alone is capable of meeting the conditions of the Law that binds us to another family member. Christ alone can pay the price of redemption. Christ alone will take upon Himself our debt and settle the legal claims against us and bring us into His family as His chosen Bride.

Wait, beloved . . . sit still.

Am I writing to any patient people? People who naturally, calmly sit still while waiting for something important?

Frankly, I hate missing the elevator. Here at church, I've discovered that when I get on the elevator to go up to the second floor, if I push the number and then immediately push the "Close door" button, the doors close at least two seconds faster. Of course, people trying to get on the elevator get smushed, but that's their problem. Besides, they need to learn a little patience.

I always dreaded the comment section on my elementary school report card. We got our grade in one column and then, there was that awful column where the teacher could make comments under headings like "Self-control." For some odd, tortuous reason, my parents took that section much more seriously than the grades. This was a no-win for me.

The comments were always, "Stevie needs to sit still; Stevie talks too much in class; Stevie disturbs his classmates; Stevie needs to exercise more self-control."

Listen, how does a kid wait patiently when he knows recess is almost here . . . or lunch . . . or gym class . . . or, for that fact, Christmas morning. There's some exciting stuff ahead and the last thing we want to do is *sit still.*

I really haven't improved very much over the years. Well, maybe a little, only because it's just harder to move as fast. Frankly, this is my ongoing challenge in life, and maybe yours, as well.

Wait . . . surrender . . . sit, while your Redeemer is at work. The imperative form of this Hebrew verb *sebi* also conveys the idea *stay put* . . . and, even, *stay calm.*[7]

Now you're really pushing it! It's one thing to stay put—it's another thing to stay calm!

The verb is used of a farmer who awaits the growth of his crops. And what good will it do a farmer to pace in his cornfield. He's done all he can do and the rest is in the hands of God.

The challenge of sitting still and staying calm boils down to trust . . . surrendering to whatever the hand of God will soon deliver. And in that surrender we actually find the strength to sit still.

The basis for Ruth staying put is in Naomi's correct summation:

    [T]*he man* [Boaz] ***will not rest until he has settled it today***
    (Ruth 3:18*b*).

Ruth can wait because Boaz won't.

Ruth can rest because Boaz isn't about to.

Ruth can sit still because Boaz is doing anything *but* sitting still. He's racing off to arrange for the redemption of his bride.

One author provoked my thinking to consider passages in the Bible where the word *still* is found.[8]

You have this text here in **Ruth 3:18** which can be translated *sit still.* I found not only that expression but *stand still* (Exodus 14:13 NKJV).

You may remember that fascinating scene where the Israelites had exited Egypt following the final plague which took the lives of the first-born throughout the land. The people of Israel rushed out in their new-found freedom.

But Pharaoh had a change of heart and, in a violent rage, he commanded his 600 chariots, plus every other available chariot in the land and every soldier to ride out and pursue Israel.

Israel was camped on the edge of the Red Sea—not the "Reed" Sea, which liberals love to say, where you can wade across. This is the Red Sea which feeds off the Indian Ocean and is, on average, 1,700 feet deep. That's why we call this a miracle. It's further proven by the sheer panic of the Israelites; they knew they were cornered and awaiting annihilation.

And God said to the people of Israel, through Moses,

> *"Stand still and see the salvation of the LORD which He will accomplish for you today"* (Exodus 14:13 NKJV).

The phrase *stand still* appears again where Job is told to *"stand still and consider the wondrous works of God"* (Job 37:14). Deeply discouraged and desperately ill, Job is told to patiently surrender to the sovereign will of God—to *stand still* and take note of the marvel of God's creation.

Sit still . . . stand still . . . be still.

When the people were troubled over their national sin during their revival under the leadership of Nehemiah, the Levites calmed the people with the promise of their forgiveness:

> *"Be still, for the day is holy; do not be grieved"* (Nehemiah 8:11).

When tempted to sin, the Psalmist David advised the reader to ***be still*** (Psalm 4:4*c*).

When troubled by the corruption of the world and the long delay of God to do anything on behalf of the believer, David writes,

> *Be still before the LORD and wait patiently for Him; do not fret when men succeed in their ways* (Psalm 37:7 NIV).

Of course, the classic passage you've probably already thought of is where David quotes the counsel of God:

> *"Be still and know that I am God. I will be exalted among the heathen; I will be exalted in the earth"* (Psalm 46:10 KJV).

I love the way David ties together our ability to be still in the prayer he crafts:

> *O God, do not remain quiet . . . and, O God, do not be still* (Psalm 83:1).

The believer can sit still, stand still, and be still because our Redeemer does *not* sit still, He does *not* stand still, and He will *not* be still.

Even now, Christ is unceasingly:

- interceding *for* the believer *(Hebrews 8:1)*;
- at work *in* the believer *(Philippians 2:13)*;
- arranging all things together for His good purposes *on behalf of* the believer *(Romans 8:28)*.

Sit still, stand still and be still—because God isn't.

Ruth, you can wait, rest, and trust; your beloved is at work to win you. The tale of God's provision and power isn't over . . . the best is yet to come!

I remember reading words I could easily picture in my mind. An author wrote of those early days in his life when, as a little boy, he would curl up in the back of the family car as his father drove home through the night. He talked of how he felt so safe tucked back there, with Dad in the driver's seat. But, he recalled, sometimes his grandmother would be with them and she would sit on the edge of that front seat, instructing his father every five minutes: "Watch the side of the road there . . . be careful of that driver coming up next to us . . . don't drive so fast."

He concluded that his grandmother never *enjoyed* the ride because she didn't trust his father. And because she couldn't trust his driving, she couldn't rest in the journey.

Powerful stuff.

But the author added one more convicting thought: "Grandmother and I both reached our destination at the same time. But one of us got there with frazzled nerves, while the other arrived happy and rested. The difference was a matter of trust."

By the way, Naomi didn't give Ruth the counsel to *sit still* because it was easy to apply or obey. Frankly, this advice is never easy . . . but it is possible.

It's a matter of trust when it comes to sitting, standing, remaining still . . . or riding in the back seat. Our response to the difficulty of our circumstances is directly related to the depth of our confidence in God's driving ability.

Nothing under His control can ever be out of control.[9]

So, just how are we to sit still and stay put and wait? How do we wait for that phone call . . . that acceptance letter . . . that doctor's report . . . that invitation . . . that contract . . . that delivery . . . that surgery . . . that arrival . . . that decision?

I've heard the average person will spend three years of his life waiting in line. So how do we handle a lifetime of waiting?

We begin with a fresh vision of the care and concern of our Beloved Redeemer. And let's not forget that He can fulfill His promises without our help. That doesn't mean we don't do anything. It means that we understand that worrying over what we can't do is nothing less than a lack of trust in what only God can do.

And that's when you sit still . . . stand still . . . be still, and get ready to know in a deeper way that *He* is God.

It occurred to me that every Christian is going to arrive at the creation of the new heaven and the new earth at the same time. Even those of us who drive faster won't get there quicker. I wonder how many of us will have gotten any joy out of the journey . . . any sense of peace in His abilities and His timing.

So, pull up a chair and sit with Ruth. Perhaps the most poignant verse in this entire book, so far, is **"Wait** [sit still]**, my daughter until you know how the matter turns out"** (Ruth 3:18a).

Rest assured—your Redeemer is at work today. To me the great lesson here, beneath the superficial and the temporary, is this truth: we simply need a fresh vision of our Redeemer's ability.

Be still is directly related to knowing *that He is God.*

> *Be Thou my Vision, O Lord of my heart—*
> *Naught be all else to me, save that Thou art;*
> *Thou my best thought, by day or by night—*
> *Waking or sleeping, Thy presence my light.*
>
> *Be Thou my Wisdom, and Thou my true Word—*
> *I ever with Thee and Thou with me, Lord;*
> *Thou my great Father, I Thy true son—*
> *Thou in me dwelling, and I with Thee one.*
>
> *High King of heaven, my victory won,*
> *May I reach heaven's joys, O bright heaven's Sun!*
> *Heart of my own heart, whatever befall,*
> *Still be my Vision, O Ruler of all.*[10]

With fresh insight, let's gain new confidence as we curl up in the back seat and rely on God, in the driver's seat, to bring us to the chosen places of His desire . . . and our delight.

Now Boaz went up to the gate and sat down there, and behold, the close relative of whom Boaz spoke was passing by, so he said, "Turn aside, friend, sit down here." And he turned aside and sat down. ²He took ten men of the elders of the city and said, "Sit down here." So they sat down. ³Then he said to the closest relative, "Naomi, who has come back from the land of Moab, has to sell the piece of land which belonged to our brother Elimelech. ⁴So I thought to inform you, saying, 'Buy it before those who are sitting here, and before the elders of my people. If you will redeem it, redeem it; but if not, tell me that I may know; for there is no one but you to redeem it, and I am after you.'" And he said, "I will redeem it." ⁵Then Boaz said, "On the day you buy the field from the hand of Naomi, you must also acquire Ruth the Moabitess, the widow of the deceased, in order to raise up the name of the deceased on his inheritance." ⁶The closest relative said, "I cannot redeem it for myself, because I would jeopardize my own inheritance. Redeem it for yourself; you may have my right of redemption, for I cannot redeem it."

⁷Now this was the custom in former times in Israel concerning the redemption and the exchange of land to confirm any matter: a man removed his sandal and gave it to another; and this was the manner of attestation in Israel. ⁸So the closest relative said to Boaz, "Buy it for yourself." And he removed his sandal. ⁹Then Boaz said to the elders and all the people, "You are witnesses today that I have bought from the hand of Naomi all that belonged to Elimelech and all that belonged to Chilion and Mahlon. ¹⁰Moreover, I have acquired Ruth the Moabitess, the widow of Mahlon, to be my wife in order to raise up the name of the deceased on his inheritance, so that the name of the deceased will not be cut off from his brothers or from the court of his birth place; you are witnesses today." ¹¹All the people who were in the court, and the elders, said, "We are witnesses. May the LORD make the woman who is coming into your home like Rachel and Leah, both of whom built the house of Israel; and may you achieve wealth in Ephrathah and become famous in Bethlehem. ¹²Moreover, may your house be like the house of Perez whom Tamar bore to Judah, through the offspring which the LORD will give you by this young woman."

–Ruth 4:1–12

CHAPTER NINE

SEALED WITH A SANDAL

Ruth 4:1–12

⌒◌⌒

The Book of Ruth opens with three funerals but closes with a wedding . . . and a baby boy. There is a good deal of weeping recorded in the first chapter, but the last is filled with overflowing joy. Now, not all of life's events have a happy ending, but this little book reminds the Christian, especially, that it is God who writes the last chapter.[1]

And in this particular book, the last chapter couldn't be more dramatically different from the first.

When we began our study through the Book of Ruth, I referred to the fact that most dads have spent quite a bit of time reading fairytales to their little girls. Those old fairytales were the best. And if you recall, eventually the prince would have to do something heroic. Whether it was to climb a tower or search the kingdom or slay a dragon . . . sooner or later, the prince *had* to take charge.

My daughters wanted their daily dose of fairytale excitement and often, before bedtime, they asked me to read a story from one of their large, colorful books. I'd pull their leg by saying, "Tell you what, I'll make up a fairytale tonight." They'd giggle in delight at the thought of a homespun story.

Then I would simply say, "Once upon a time . . . the end," and lay my head back on the chair as if to go to sleep.

"Daddy, that's not a *real* story. You can't tell a story with "Once upon a time" and "The end" so close together . . . you gotta have something in the *middle*."

I'm afraid we, especially older Christians who've read all the stories before, tend to treat the Bible like that:

- You remember when Esther became the queen? Yeah, she won the contest and then saved her people! *Um* . . . what happened in the middle?

- You remember when Daniel went to Babylon? Yep, he was thrown into the lion's den? But what happened in between?

- You remember when Jesus went to the cross? Oh, yes, and He rose again. True, but what happened before that?

- You remember the story of Ruth? Uh-huh, she was a widow and Boaz married her . . . isn't that great?!

That's like saying, "Once upon a time . . . the end." Not so fast . . . we still need to hear about the prince riding in to rescue the fair damsel.

One of the most intriguing scenes in this drama is at the city gate, where Boaz challenged the other potential redeemer in a strategic battle of wits.

Thus far, we've observed three months of courtship and a midnight proposal. Boaz and Ruth have whispered of their love out there on the threshing floor.

But we also discovered a problem—a big one. There is *another* prince who has the legal right to the fair princess. This is where it really gets interesting.

> **Now Boaz went up to the gate and sat down there, and behold, the close relative of whom Boaz spoke was passing by, so he said, "Turn aside, friend, sit down here." And he turned aside and sat down. He took ten men of the elders of the city and said, "Sit down here." So they sat down** (Ruth 4:1–2).

The city gate was literally the open area inside the town entrance where business was generally transacted.[2] It was at the gate where elders sat and heard legal cases and passed legal judgment. It was at the city gate where civil plans were discussed. What was decided at the gate was the *final* word.[3]

By the way, this illuminates what Jesus Christ meant when He promised His disciples *"I will build my church and the gates of Hades will not overpower it"* (Matthew 16:18). In other words, all the plans and schemes and decisions and even the final word of hell will never crush the Church.

Perhaps you noticed that Boaz has invited ten elders to sit down and hear out this matter. Ten elders was the minimum number needed for a quorum for a legal proceeding. So, as soon as Boaz meets the quorum, he's ready to go.

And at just that moment, the other kinsman redeemer *just so happens* to walk by. Obviously, Samuel wants us to know that God is providentially arranging the details—above and beyond what Boaz is capable of thinking through:

> **Then he said to the closest relative** [literally: the goel/
> redeemer] **"Naomi, who has come back from the land of
> Moab, has to sell the piece of land which belonged to our
> brother Elimelech"** (Ruth 4:3).

Most believe the word "brother" in this context is a broad term indicating clan relation, rather than an immediate family member. In other words, the land belonged to the clan of Elimelech.

These are the opening lines of Boaz. Paraphrased in our vernacular, Boaz would have been casually informing this older man, "Hey, you know that piece of land Naomi inherited from her deceased husband—well, she can't do anything with it on account of the fact that her sons also died. Well, you're the next in line, so if you want it, you ought to go ahead and buy it."

If Boaz was a poker player, he would win at every hand. Not that I know anything about poker, I'm just saying . . . in fact, I can't even play Rook all that well. My girls loved tearing me to shreds. Part of my problem was that whenever I got a good hand, everybody knew it. They could read the sheer delight all over my face . . . everybody knew: Daddy just got lots of one color . . . or the Rook!

Not Boaz . . . he's as cool as a cucumber, even with his heart threatening to leap out of his chest! He continues:

> **"So I thought to inform you, saying, 'Buy it before those
> who are sitting here, and before the elders of my people. If**

you will redeem it, redeem it; but if not, tell me that I may know; for there is no one but you to redeem it, and I am after you'" (Ruth 4:4*a*).

Again, paraphrased, "I just thought I'd let you know I'm interested in that land, as well . . . so, if you want it, go ahead and buy it, since you're first in line. But if you don't want it, well, I might as well buy it for myself."

Have you ever tried to mask your emotions as you've interviewed for a job you really wanted. It offers twice the pay, three times the vacation, and a company car. On the outside, you're low-key and composed during the interview. But on the inside, you're down on your knees begging, "Please, give me this job." And at the end of the interview, when they say, "We'll hire you. When can you start?" you say, "Well, let me check my calendar."

On the outside, Boaz is feigning only the slightest interest. On the inside, Boaz is begging, "Please don't redeem this property." The truth is Boaz already assumed this man would agree to buy the land.

And that's exactly why he started the discussion about the land without mentioning the two widows who came with it. Boaz wanted the last bit of news to be placed negatively in such a way as to overpower the positive aspect of available land for sale.

In the same way, someone will say to you, "Which do you want first: the good news or the bad news?" You normally respond with, "Give me the *bad* news first." Why? Because you know that no matter how bad it is, good news is just around the corner and it will more than likely compensate for the bad news.

Boaz reverses the order—he starts with the good news. He was shrewd, knowing that the bad news that follows will probably overshadow the good news and render it negative.

"Hey, a piece of land just came on the market and you've got first dibs on it . . . you interested?" And the man answers, *"I will redeem it"* (Ruth 4:4*b*).

I'm sure Boaz's heart skipped a beat . . . but from studying his strategy, I believe he fully expected it. Now watch this—Boaz continues:

"On the day you buy the field from the hand of Naomi, you must also acquire Ruth the Moabitess, the widow of the

***deceased, in order to raise up the name of the deceased on
his inheritance"*** (Ruth 4:5).

What incredible strategy. Sure enough, this potential redeemer hadn't
thought about Naomi or Ruth. Boaz eliminates any enthusiasm this man
might have had over a good land deal by laying out the bad news, one piece
at a time.

Let's read verse five again, a little slower, as this other guy would have
heard it; let it sink in:

- ***On the day you buy the field from the hand of Naomi, you must*** –
  I must?!

- ***also redeem Ruth*** – Who's she?

- ***the Moabitess*** – No! Our ancient enemies—pagan idolaters!

- ***the widow of the deceased*** – What? She's been married? And I'm
  supposed to marry her when I buy the land?

- ***in order to raise up the name of the deceased*** – I'm responsible to
  give her an heir? I'll have a half-Gentile child!

- to raise him up ***on his inheritance*** – You mean I have to give the
  child this piece of land I just bought, as *his* inheritance?!

Let me paraphrase the bad news that Boaz just delivered: "Oh, and
by the way, if you redeem the land, you'll have to care for a widow named
Naomi, as well as marry her widowed Moabitess daughter-in-law and give
her an heir that you name after her first husband . . . and when the boy
reaches manhood, you will, according to Mosaic law, give him that piece of
property as his inheritance. So whatever you buy today, you're going to have
to give away later. Just thought you might want to know all of that before
you seal the deal."

As quickly as this guy said, "I'll buy it," he's now looking for a fire escape.
If he purchases the land:

He has to care for Naomi.

He has to marry a foreign woman from Moab.

He has to raise a child with this Gentile widow.

He has to give away the land to that child.

He will *lose* whatever he's invested in the property.

And the son he might have with Ruth will not even have his name but the name of his wife's deceased husband!

Who in his right mind would want to do such a thing? There's only one person willing to do any of that: someone in love with the widow! *That* overrules everything.

So, what happens next?

> *The closest relative said, "I cannot redeem it for myself, because I would jeopardize my own inheritance"* (Ruth 4:6*a*).

That's the long way around saying, "There's no way I want to do all that . . . besides, I don't want to ruin my own financial standing with a purchase that becomes a debt. And I certainly don't want to mix my clan with Gentile offspring . . . especially from a Moabitess . . . the deal's off."

Then he went on to say the words that Boaz was hoping so desperately to hear:

> *"Redeem it for yourself; you may have my right of redemption, for I cannot redeem it"* (Ruth 4:6*b*).

And for the second time Boaz shouts "*Yeeeeehaw!*" You'll just have to take my word on that.

The decision is ratified in their traditional manner:

> *Now this was the custom in former times in Israel concerning the redemption and the exchange of land to confirm any matter: a man removed his sandal and gave it to another; and this was the manner of attestation in Israel. So the closest relative said to Boaz, "Buy it for yourself." And he removed his sandal* (Ruth 4:7–8).

Why did he give Boaz his sandal? In the Old Testament, shoes and feet symbolized ownership and possession. The Lord gave mankind the rule over creation, and David the psalmist put it this way:

> *You* [God] *have put all things under his* [man's] *feet* (Psalm 8:6).

The people of Israel were told by the Lord *every place on which the sole of your foot treads shall be yours* (Deuteronomy 11:24). The reverse was just as meaningful. In *Exodus 3:5*, when Moses met with God at the burning bush, God had him to remove his sandals as a symbol that Moses owned nothing but God owned everything.[4]

So when this near relative took off his sandal and gave it to Boaz, he symbolized that he was not going to own that property—his feet wouldn't walk on that land, so to speak. The sandal transfer indicated this transfer of power. He was literally saying, "Boaz, you can walk in my sandals; you can walk the path in my place."

And that also meant that Boaz could walk down the wedding aisle in this man's place and take Ruth as his bride:

> ***Then Boaz said to the elders and all the people, "You are witnesses today that I have bought from the hand of Naomi all that belonged to Elimelech and all that belonged to Chilion and Mahlon. Moreover, I have acquired Ruth the Moabitess, the widow of Mahlon, to be my wife in order to raise up the name of the deceased on his inheritance, so that the name of the deceased will not be cut off from his brothers or from the court of his birth place; you are witnesses today"*** (Ruth 4:9–10).

Boaz wants to make sure the legal language is recorded in the minutes of the town meeting. He has a quorum of elders and witnesses from among the people who've gathered around. He doesn't want any misunderstanding later. He repeats every possible detail, including all the names of the parties involved.

Can you imagine how the other kinsman redeemer feels right about now, knowing that Boaz had planned for this outcome all along! But it didn't matter . . . he didn't want his name or family inheritance jeopardized!

By the way, do you know the name of this barefoot redeemer? No? Well, neither does anyone else. The man who didn't want to endanger his name through marriage to Ruth; the man who wanted to protect his name from Gentile blood; the man who avoided God's intention within His law of redemption . . . his name has been *forgotten.*

Do you think Boaz ruined his name or reputation? Not on your life. In fact, years after Boaz and Ruth died, when Solomon built that massive temple to God's glory, two bronze columns stood freely on the outer porch—one on the left, the other on the right—and every man and woman who walked between them could see the names of two men etched into them . . . names whose meanings represented the character of God . . . men who had lived out godly character. One of the names etched into those two columns was the name Boaz.

Throughout history the story of a prince named Boaz and a princess named Ruth lives on.

And now all the people respond with prophetic precision:

> *All the people who were in the court, and the elders, said, "We are witnesses. May the LORD make the woman who is coming into your home like Rachel and Leah, both of whom built the house of Israel; and may you achieve wealth in Ephrathah and become famous in Bethlehem"* (Ruth 4:11).

These people have *no* idea how their blessing will one day come true. Ruth will become the great-grandmother of King David. Boaz and Ruth will continue the line through which our Lord Jesus Christ will come—the great Kinsman Redeemer.

Unfortunately, we're not given any details of the wedding, the wedding garments, the feasting, or the days of celebration. It simply tells us that the bride and groom were together at last.

The prince has rescued the princess.

But I've wondered why this godly Jewish man would be interested in a foreign widow. Why would a godly man like Boaz imperil his good name by linking it to a Moabitess, having children who are half-Jew and half-Gentile, having his name whispered that he was the man who married a former idolater.

Why would this prince risk his reputation?

Obviously, Boaz trusted Ruth's commitment to Israel's God. She had not converted to her faith for position or money or advantage. In fact, following after God had meant that Ruth walked away from every possible source of security.

The virtue of her testimony was the appealing factor to Boaz. But she also reminded him of someone. Boaz already knew the testimony of a Gentile woman who had left her country and her heritage and her idols to follow after the God of Abraham.

His own mother.

Boaz's mother had followed after Israel, converting from idolatry to faith in the true and living God after the walls of Jericho fell before the Israelites.

Later, a Jewish man by the name of Salmon married his mother—that foreign Gentile woman with a past. They would appear in the genealogy of Jesus Christ, listed in *Matthew 1*.

Boaz was willing to do the very same thing his father had done years before. He was not deterred by Ruth's past. He knew the testimony of his mother, who'd left her sinful past as a prostitute and devoted the rest of her life to the laws of God's holiness and purity. He had heard that testimony from his mother's own lips as she explained how she had been known throughout the city of Jericho as one of the resident harlots. He knew the pain it had caused her and the gratitude she felt for God's grace.

Boaz also knew that his father had been willing to risk *his* good name by marrying a woman with a past but, more importantly, a woman with a heart devoted to God.

Like father, like son.

Think of it; Boaz isn't afraid to trust his future children to the care of a former Gentile idolater because he was a child raised by a former Gentile idolater: the woman listed in *Matthew 1* and *Hebrews 11* as Rahab the harlot.

Isn't it wonderful to see how God prepared Boaz's heart to love a Gentile bride and become her kinsman redeemer?

Don't forget, your Kinsman Redeemer Jesus Christ redeems people with a past. In fact, He has chosen a Bride that carries both Jewish and Gentile blood—a bride composed of every tribe, tongue, and nation *(Revelation 5:9)*.

Jesus Christ is a mixed breed, too. Our Kinsman Redeemer descended from Rahab . . . and Ruth.

And His love for us has not sullied His name, yet. It has not jeopardized His reputation—it has only enhanced it with undiminished beauty.

He is the Kinsman Redeemer of grace!

¹³So Boaz took Ruth, and she became his wife, and he went in to her. And the LORD enabled her to conceive, and she gave birth to a son. ¹⁴Then the women said to Naomi, "Blessed is the LORD who has not left you without a redeemer today, and may his name become famous in Israel. ¹⁵May he also be to you a restorer of life and a sustainer of your old age; for your daughter-in-law, who loves you and is better to you than seven sons, has given birth to him."

¹⁶Then Naomi took the child and laid him in her lap, and became his nurse. ¹⁷The neighbor women gave him a name, saying, "A son has been born to Naomi!" So they named him Obed. He is the father of Jesse, the father of David.

¹⁸Now these are the generations of Perez: to Perez was born Hezron, ¹⁹and to Hezron was born Ram, and to Ram, Amminadab, ²⁰and to Amminadab was born Nahshon, and to Nahshon, Salmon, ²¹and to Salmon was born Boaz, and to Boaz, Obed, ²²and to Obed was born Jesse, and to Jesse, David.

–Ruth 4:13–22

CHAPTER TEN

AND THEY LIVED HAPPILY EVER AFTER!

Ruth 4:13–22

At the beginning of nearly every fairytale I used to read to my little girls were the words, "Once upon a time . . ." That line alone conjures up memories of damsels in distress, evil enemies, desperate times, and a courageous prince saving the day and rescuing the princess.

"Once upon a time" really did happen! A damsel in distress was really and truly rescued by a prince of a man.

Not only would this prince and princess be given a part to play in the genealogy of the Messiah, they would become a model of virtue and purity and obedience to God for their generation . . . and beyond.

Even though we're dealing with imperfect people who are sinners and in need of God's grace throughout life, it's obvious that Boaz and Ruth followed after God *before* and *after* they married.

They not only remained faithful to each other, they raised a godly son who continued the legacy of faith—a legacy that stretched all the way down to their most famous descendant: their great-grandson David, the poet-king of Israel.

Let's watch as this wonderful true-to-life fairytale wraps up with some often-overlooked, yet wonderful, scenes.

A WEDDING CEREMONY
CONSUMMATED

So Boaz took Ruth, and she became his wife, and he went in to her. And the LORD enabled her to conceive, and she gave birth to a son (Ruth 4:13).

You can't help but notice how quickly this dramatic tale comes to a close. In 29 words—two sentences—you have a wedding; a honeymoon; a home established; a marriage consummated; a baby conceived; nine months of anticipation; a healthy boy delivered.

If we slow it down and climb back into this scene, the wedding ceremony alone would have been an elaborate affair. The entire town would have been invited.

The bride and groom would be dressed as much like a king and queen as those times allowed. If the groom were rich—Boaz was—he wore a headpiece or crown made of gold. It was also the custom of the groom to have his garments scented with two special fragrances—frankincense and myrrh—which foretold his future descendant, our Kinsman Redeemer, Who was presented with gifts befitting someone who had come to redeem a Bride.

For Boaz and Ruth, their marriage was consummated, and a few brief words later we're told she gives birth to a son:

The neighbor women gave him a name, saying, "A son has been born to Naomi!" So they named him Obed. He is the father of Jesse, the father of David (Ruth 4:17).

It's certainly unusual for the women in the village to name the child; they may have very well come up with the name in their excitement and Boaz and Ruth agreed to it.

You'll notice in these closing verses that Boaz and Ruth effectively disappear and the interest of the Scripture returns to Naomi.[1] It seems that Samuel, the author, wants to end the story by focusing the lens of Scripture where he began.

A WIDOWED GRANDMOTHER
INVIGORATED

Then the women said to Naomi, "Blessed is the LORD who has not left you without a redeemer today, and may his name become famous in Israel. May he also be to you a restorer of life and a sustainer of your old age; for your daughter-in-law, who [by the way] **loves you, and is better to you than seven sons, has given birth to him"** (Ruth 4:14–15).

They are observing, "Naomi, because of Ruth and your grandson, you are now surrounded by care and protection and love . . . and this grandbaby is restoring your life and giving you energy and joy in your old age!"

Not only do we observe a wedding ceremony consummated, we have a widowed grandmother invigorated. What an incredible reversal. This book opened with sorrow and ends with satisfaction.

Naomi had been taken by her husband with their two sons to Moab. It was an act of disobedience on the part of Elimelech, who died, along with his two grown sons. Naomi found herself traveling back to Bethlehem with little hope of physically surviving, much less finding happiness again.

What's more, there is no heir to her husband's estate. Everything she owned in Bethlehem will go to the highest bidder. She will spend the rest of her life alongside her daughter-in-law, foraging for a living. She even changed her name to Bitterness and assumed that God had abandoned her, too.

But now look at her: she's in the home of a leading prince, the husband of her daughter-in-law and, if that isn't good enough, she's now holding a grandson in her lap. Samuel says **[t]hen Naomi took the child and laid him in her lap, and became his nurse** (Ruth 4:16). You could render that word *nurse* as guardian . . . caregiver.

No wonder the women are all saying to her, "This little boy is further proof that your life has been restored. This little grandson is going to put a bounce back in your step; he's going to wind the clock back and reinvigorate your mind and heart."

You'd better believe this is one invigorated grandmother! What a thrill for her to dedicate her final years to the task of helping Ruth and Boaz raise this boy in a godly fashion.

Warren Wiersbe, commenting on Naomi's joy in this text and writing as a proud grandparent himself noted, "Grandchildren are better than the Fountain of Youth, for we get young again when the grandchildren come to visit." [2]

I'm a new grandparent, and I'm ready for that unique opportunity to grow young again! And I'm really looking forward to enjoying children without being responsible for their actions.

Someone wrote that children and their grandparents are natural allies. [3] Isn't that the truth? Have you ever been to Cracker Barrel and seen one of those "Grandmother Paddles" for spanking grandchildren? It's a long stick with a soft cushion at the other end . . . that says it all! Mom and Dad are struggling through the daily chores of civilizing their little barbarians and Grandma comes along and says, "Look at my little angels." And Mom and Dad are thinking, *Fallen angels.*

One guy asked a mother, "If you had it to do all over, would you have children again?" She said, "Yes, but not the same ones."

Grandparents can't understand that . . . their grandchildren are perfect little people . . . which is why grandparents are blind to the things their grandkids get away with. Maybe that's why they don't see the spilled cereal or the muddy tracks on the floor—they don't seem bothered that the kids ate dessert first . . . or that's the *only* thing they ate.

Here's what's really happening in Naomi's life: she's reveling in the grace of God; she's basking in the goodness of God, which is revealed in a roof over her head, food in her stomach, an heir to her late husband's property, a kinsman redeemer, and a grandbaby to receive all the love and affection she's bottled up for years.

One medical doctor who authored a number of books on the subject of grandparenting wrote that the bond between a child and a grandparent is the least complicated form of human love. [4]

Frankly, any child who has that relationship is blessed. My grandmother on my mother's side lived in my hometown. She also served in the Servicemen's Center in Norfolk, Virginia—the flagship center for Missions to Military, which my parents founded in 1958. Every Friday night, my entire family went downtown to the Center for Bible study, food and, for us missionary kids, a lot of fun times playing games.

The Center was a large three-story building with everything from bunk rooms, library, kitchen, and study area to game rooms with ping pong, shuffle board, and table games galore. There was a counter topped with cookies and a soda fountain to which we had free access.

We looked forward to Friday night.

And just about every Friday night, one of us four boys went home with Granny—that's what we called her—to spend the night at her house. She had been widowed for many years and had dedicated the rest of her life to serving as a missionary to these young navy guys docked in Norfolk.

Spending the night at her little house was always icing on the cake. For one thing, she had a television. We did, too, when we were older, but we were rarely allowed to watch anything but football games and "Daniel Boone." Our home TV never operated without static/fuzz, and we had to change the channel with a pair of pliers.

But that once-a-month sleepover at Granny's house meant staying in our pajamas and watching Saturday morning cartoons while eating our own box of cereal—our choice! None of those Bran Flakes—you know, the best value for your money—oh, no, my choice was always Cap'n Crunch.

You might think Cap'n Crunch wasn't around in 1968. It was; in fact in 1967, Crunch Berries came out and then Peanut Butter Crunch debuted in 1969. I know what I'm talking about . . . Cap'n Crunch has been ruining kids' teeth for almost fifty years.

But there's more to this unbridled tale: Granny let us have a cup of coffee!

Shocking, I know. And my parents knew it, too. But they wisely figured that once a month away from chores and homework and the normal disciplines of a frugal life were not going to ruin us for good.

Granny certainly bent a digestive rule or two . . . and we loved it. But be careful with this story, grandparents—there's a fine line between allowing cartoons and Cap'n Crunch and compromising moral standards or ignoring disobedience to Christ in your response to their behavior.

Frankly, what I remember most about those sleepovers was that after breakfast time was finished and the coffee cup was drained, Granny would come over and sit next to me and open her Bible. She'd read a chapter and then preach a little sermon to me about how I needed to follow Christ and give Him my life. And then she would pray. The longest prayer you can imagine.

She prayed around the world; she prayed for lost people she was witnessing to and new sailors she had led to Christ; she prayed for other missionaries we supported and the churches that supported us all; and then . . . she prayed for me.

She did nothing but complement my parents' desire to see me grow up to follow Christ. My grandmother prayed for me until she finally lost her mental capacities and eventually went home to be with the Lord.

So when I read this little phrase about Obed being taken into the care of Naomi, don't miss what it probably meant to him . . . and to her.

A grandparent has the ability to impact grandchildren in so many ways:

- offer an emotional and, perhaps, physical safety net when parents fail or falter;

- teach the plan of salvation; Timothy learned the Gospel from his mother *and* his grandmother *(2 Timothy 1:5)*;

- be a unique witness of how God has been faithful to their family over the years; the memorial stones on the banks of the Jordan served as a storybook for grandparents to retell the story of God's faithfulness to the children of Israel *(Joshua 4)*;

- be a wise counselor with years of experience and biblical knowledge;

- be a non-judgmental counselor as the grandchildren share difficult questions and experiences;

- be a place of refuge and comfort for grandchildren who feel that there's no one else they can confide in with trust and confidence other than Mom and Dad;

- understand the significance of milestones in a child's life; they don't get bogged down with the details so much as they cheer their grandchildren along.

We all need to pay attention to this subject of grandparenting and its growing potential and influence in the world. I've read that half of the adult population over the age of 45 is now a grandparent and 83 percent of people aged 60 and older are grandparents—we now have more than 75 million grandparents in America. In fact, by the turn of this century, at least 4 million children were already living in a grandparent's home.[5]

I wonder, out of the myriad of books on parenting, where are the books providing advice for godly grandparenting? Well, here's a great text and context for providing some excellent tips.

Naomi could offer her grandson something that Ruth could not. As a new convert, Ruth knew nothing of Jewish customs and traditions in the home. Ruth had so much to learn from the Law of Moses and the history of God's people; she barely had time to learn herself before Obed began asking all those hard questions.

What a wonderful asset Naomi provided Boaz and Ruth in raising their son to follow after God. Don't ever forget that parents *and* grandparents can play different, but essential, roles.

A WONDERFUL KINSMAN REDEEMER ANTICIPATED

The Book of Ruth ends as quickly as it began. You have the genealogical record of descendants:

> *You have Perez, the father of Hezron, and Hezron is the father of Ram, and Ram the father of Amminadab, and Amminadab is the father of Nahshon, and Nahshon fathers Salmon, and Salmon fathers Boaz, and Boaz is the father of Obed, and to Obed was born Jesse, and to Jesse, David* (paraphrased).

If you read that slowly enough, you're struck by the fact that Ruth, the Moabitess widow, the once impoverished gleaner in the fields of Bethlehem, has become the great-grandmother of King David!

And it is quite possible that she lived long enough to see him born. But that's not really the end of the story. Wouldn't you like to know a little more about them? I would.

So what's *the rest of the story*?

Paul Harvey was a news commentator who, for fifty years, enthralled people with the inside scoop on current and historical events. For decades he narrated a radio piece called "The Rest of the Story."

. He told the story of Dick and Alvah, who worked together selling and repairing watches in the late 1800s. Before long their business expanded and they ventured into selling other items, eventually printing a booklet—a catalog, they called it—so their clients could order without ever having to leave home. Dick and Alvah even opened a few stores and began to sell a variety of goods. Their business quickly flourished but so did the debts. Alvah became concerned that he might be held personally liable in a bankruptcy, so he sold his share to Dick in 1894 for $20,000.

A depression hit in 1907 and sales declined. Dick sold his shares in 1909 for 10 million dollars and retired. The name of the business remained the same, with both men's names on the store fronts. Dick died in 1914, a multi-millionaire, while Allen—though never poor—did not have the financial success of his former partner. His retirement was interrupted by the Great Depression, which led him to return to the company as sort of a historical icon, making heavily advertised visits as late as the early 1940s to stores across America that bore the name of these two men: Dick Sears and Alvah Roebuck.

And now you know the rest of the story.

Personally, I'd like to know more about this eternally significant story between Boaz and Ruth. I'd love to know a little more about the rest of *their* story.

With that in mind, I'll begin with Ruth 5:1:

> *And so it came to pass that Boaz and Ruth were married in the presence of many witnesses. The wedding guests came from all around Judea to add their blessings to the union and future home of Boaz and Ruth.*
>
> *The morning after all the guests had departed, Boaz awakened while it was still early. He looked throughout the house and could not find Ruth anywhere. He began to search diligently for her outside, and upon entering his fields, he saw his bride gleaning there.*
>
> *Once again, she was dressed in rough clothing and her sack for grain was about her shoulders.*
>
> *"Ruth!" he called as he ran to her. "Ruth, why are you gleaning in the fields today?" She bowed low to the ground and said, "My*

husband, surely I must find something to satisfy the hunger I will have today."

Upon hearing this, Boaz embraced Ruth in his arms and said, "Ruth, understand that since you have become my bride, all that belongs to me belongs to you."

Okay, I made all that up! I hope you didn't take your Bible and thumb through Ruth looking for chapter five.

But it occurred to me—and I imagined the above—isn't this the point of their story? Boaz is a picture of our Kinsman Redeemer Who has taken *us* into the family of God, and everything that belongs to Him *now* belongs to His beloved Bride.

[He has given us] *an inheritance which is imperishable and undefiled and will not fade away* (1 Peter 1:4).

The rest of their story is told in the New Testament description of the *final* Kinsman Redeemer. So before we wrap up the love story of Boaz and Ruth, let's compare Ruth's kinsman redeemer with Christ our Redeemer, pointing out four similarities between Boaz and Christ.

Kinship with the Bride Was Required

In order to meet the conditions of the Law and qualify to redeem the bride, the kinsman redeemer had to be biologically related to the bride—a member of her kin or clan.

Likewise, Jesus Christ became our relative: a member of the human race. In order to redeem us, He wore the sandals of humanity and walked among us. John writes,

And the Word became flesh and dwelt among us (John 1:14).

Jesus became a member of the human family so that He could make us members of His royal family.

A Kinsman's Desire to Redeem His Bride Was Voluntary

The kinsman couldn't be forced; he had to be willing to redeem the bride, which means Boaz could have walked away. The other potential redeemer did. Boaz didn't. Why? Because He *loved* Ruth.

In this is love, not that we loved God, but that He loved us and sent His son to be the propitiation [satisfaction] *for our sins* (I John 4:10).

He was willing!

[W]*ho for the joy set before Him* [that joy included winning His bride] *endured the cross* (Hebrews 12:2).

He humbled Himself and became obedient to death—even death on a cross! (Philippians 2:8 NIV).

That's how willing Christ was to redeem us. He endured the cross, anticipating the joy of redeeming His bride—you and me!

Boaz was related to Ruth *and* he was willing to redeem her. Jesus Christ, related to us by flesh and blood—fully God, yet fully man—was also *willing* to redeem us, His Bride.

The Kinsman Redeemer Had to Be Capable of Paying the Redemption Price

No matter how much Boaz loved Ruth, he had to be capable of buying Elimelech's land, settling her estate, and paying off the family debts. Redeeming the bride wasn't free . . . it cost dearly!

That other near kinsman redeemer might have only needed to give Boaz his worn-out sandal to seal the covenant, but Boaz had to give him silver to settle the deal. There was no I.O.U. or "I'll see what I can do later on." Oh, no. Boaz had to have enough money to pay the debts of the widow he wanted and to buy the family property.

Fortunately Boaz was wealthy enough to take care of everything.

Listen, Bride of Christ, *you have been bought with a price* (1 Corinthians 6:20). Christ, Who is infinitely wealthy, was able to pay the price. The purchase price was not currency, though—the legal tender for our redemption was the blood of Jesus Christ. Paul wrote,

In Him we have redemption through His blood (Ephesians 1:7).

I found it interesting to discover in my study that according to Jewish custom, it was the responsibility of the kinsman redeemer to also buy out of slavery any member of the bride's family who had been forced to sell themselves to pay off their debts.[6]

A kinsman redeemer literally stepped in and settled any and all debt against his beloved. He just wiped the books clean.

So also our Lord hung on the cross and said, *"It is finished"* (John 19:30). *Tetelestai* was the Greek word He used, which literally meant *paid in full*. The debt of sin has been paid in full!

For Boaz, every single legal claim of the Law was paid; for Christ's Bride, every debt of sin attached to His beloved's name was completely paid. The debt has been wiped off the ledger.

Paul wrote,

> **[H]***aving canceled out the certificate of debt consisting of decrees against us, which was hostile to us; and He has taken it out of the way, having nailed it to the cross* (Colossians 2:14).

Jesus Christ was both willing *and* able to pay the redemption price—and He settled our debt forever.

His Provision for the Bride Was Comprehensive

Boaz lifted Ruth to his high estate. She was no longer the Moabite widow—she was the bride of Boaz. She was made a legal partaker of his name; her status was altered from "alien" to "accepted."

So also, Christ has comprehensively raised our status:

- from sinner to saint;
- from stranger to friend;
- from outcast to child;
- from lost to redeemed;
- from beggar to bride.

THE END OF THE STORY

Most fairytales I read to my girls began with the words, "Once upon a time," and nearly all of them that I can remember ended with these words: "And they lived happily ever after!"

It occurred to me that those words are an absolutely appropriate ending for every member of the Bride of Christ. Every one of us *will* live happily ever after, no matter how difficult our biography has been, no matter how muddled or challenged or painful.

At the end of our biography, after we take our last breath, our story will close with those same words: "And they lived happily ever after!" Taken away by our Prince . . . swept away by our Bridegroom . . . kept eternally in the joy of our Lord forever and ever.

But there's one more thing to note, and it is on the last page of every book I read to my girls: the words, "The end."

But not for us. For the Bride of Christ, there will *never* be an end to our "happily ever after."

We believe by faith in our Kinsman Redeemer—our Lord Jesus—and cling to His promise of grace and mercy and love and purpose, knowing that one day we will enter the glory of heaven . . . forever.

Why?

- Because He was *related* to us;

- Because He was *willing* to redeem us;

- Because He was *able* to redeem us;

- Because He was *capable* of comprehensively settling our debt of sin.

The last words on the story of the Church—the Bride of Christ, and every individual member of the bridal party—are *never* the words "The end."

Instead, they will always be . . . "And we lived happily ever after!"

ENDNOTES

CHAPTER ONE

[1] J. Vernon McGee, *Ruth: The Romance of Redemption* (Thomas Nelson, 1943), 14.

[2] A. Boyd Luter, *God Behind the Seen* (Baker Books, 1995), 14.

[3] David Shepherd, editor, *Shepherd's Notes* (Broadman & Holman, 1998), 3.

[4] McGee, 17.

[5] Ibid., 18.

[6] C.F. Keil and F. Delitzsch, *Commentary on the Old Testament: Volume 2* (Eerdmans, reprinted 1991), 494.

[7] McGee, 20.

[8] Warren W. Wiersbe, *Ruth & Esther: Be Committed* (Victor Books, 1993), 14.

CHAPTER TWO

[1] A. Boyd Luter, *Expositor's Guide to the Historical Books: God Behind the Seen* (Baker, 1995), 24.

[2] Ibid.

[3] Robert L. Hubbard, *New International Commentary on the Old Testament: The Book of Ruth* (Eerdmans, 1988), 85.

[4] C.F. Keil and F. Delitzsch, *Commentary on the Old Testament: Volume 2* (Eerdmans, reprinted 1991), 472.

[5] Hubbard, 94.

[6] Ibid.

[7] Hubbard (adapted), 91.

[8] David R. Shepherd, *Shepherd's Notes* (Broadman, 1998), 12.

[9] J. Vernon McGee (adapted), *Ruth: The Romance of Redemption* (Thomas Nelson, 1981), 53.

CHAPTER THREE

[1] citation: enotes, Thomas Jefferson, in a letter dated October 12, 1786, to Maria Cosway.

[2] Stanley Collins, *Ruth & Esther: Courage and Submission* (G/L Regal Books, 1975), 8.

[3] Robert L. Hubbard, *New International Commentary on the Old Testament: Ruth* (Eerdmans, 1988), 102.

4   Frederic W. Bush (adapted), *Word Biblical Commentary: Volume 9, Ruth* (Word Books, 1996), 75.

5   Warren W. Wiersbe, *Ruth & Esther: Be Committed* (Victor Books, 1993), 19.

6   J. Vernon McGee, *The Romance of Redemption* (Thomas Nelson, 1943), 61.

7   Collins, 11.

8   Bush, 87.

CHAPTER FOUR

1   C.F. Keil and F. Delitzsch, *Commentary on the Old Testament: Volume 2* (Eerdmans, reprinted 1991), 477.

2   Robert L. Hubbard, Jr., *New International Commentary on the Old Testament: Ruth* (Eerdmans, 1988), 133.

3   Ibid., 145.

4   Keil & Delitzsch, 477.

5   Stanley Collins, *Courage and Submission: Ruth & Esther* (Regal Books, 1975), 19.

6   J. Vernon McGee, *Ruth: The Romance of Redemption* (Thomas Nelson, reprint 1981), 81.

CHAPTER FIVE

1   *Wisconsin State Journal*, reprinted in *Parade*, citation: preachingtoday.com.

2   John Newton, "Amazing Grace" (1772; © Singspiration, Inc., 1963).

3   Robert L. Hubbard (adapted), *The Book of Ruth* (Eerdmans, 1988), 175.

4   A. Boyd Luter, *God Behind the Seen* (Baker Books, 1995), 52.

5   Warren W. Wiersbe, *Ruth & Esther: Be Committed* (Victor Books, 1993), 30.

6   Ibid., 29.

7   J. Vernon McGee, *Ruth: The Romance of Redemption* (Thomas Nelson, reprint 1981), 82.

CHAPTER SIX

1   Robert Lintzenich, *Shepherd's Notes: Ruth, Esther* (Broadman & Holman, 1998), 26.

2   J. Vernon McGee, *Ruth: The Romance of Redemption* (Thomas Nelson, 1981), 89.

3   Warren W. Wiersbe, *Ruth & Esther: Be Committed* (Victor Books, 1993), 44.

4   McGee (adapted), 91.

5   Robert L. Hubbard, Jr. *The Book of Ruth* (Eerdmans, 1988), 200.

6   Stanley Collins, *Ruth & Esther: Courage and Submission* (Regal Books, 1975), 27.

[7] A. Boyd Luter & Barry C. Davis, *Exposition of the Books of Ruth & Esther* (Baker Books, 1005), 57.

[8] Hubbard, 208.

[9] Luter & Davis, 56.

[10] C.F. Keil and F. Delitzsch, *Commentary on the Old Testament: Volume 2* (Eerdmans, Reprint, 1991), 484.

[11] Collins, 29.

[12] Hubbard, 212.

CHAPTER SEVEN

[1] Rick Holland in John MacArthur, *Right Thinking in a World Gone Wrong* (Harvest House, 2009), 30.

[2] MacArthur, 33.

[3] Ibid., 33.

[4] Ibid., 34.

[5] A. Boyd Luter & Barry C. David, *God Behind the Seen* (Baker, 1995), 62.

[6] David Nettleton, *Provision and Providence* (Regular Baptist Press, 1795), 26.

[7] M.R. De Haan, *Ruth: The Romance of Redemption* (Zondervan, 1962), 116.

[8] Michael Hodgin, *1001 More Humorous Illustrations* (Zondervan, 1998), 271.

CHAPTER EIGHT

[1] Associated Press, "Florida woman Calls 911 over McNuggets," @news.yahoo.com (3/4/09).

[2] Robert J. Morgan, *Nelson's Complete Book of Illustrations* (Thomas Nelson, 2000), 600.

[3] *The Valley of Vision* in Charles Swindoll, *Intimacy with the Almighty* (Word Publishing, 1996), 70.

[4] Robert L. Hubbard, Jr. (adapted), *The New International Commentary on the Old Testament: Ruth* (Eerdmans, 1988), 219.

[5] Stanley Collins, *Courage and Submission: A Study of Ruth & Esther* (Regal Books, 1975), 33.

[6] M.R. DeHaan, *The Romance of Redemption* (Zondervan, 1958), 119.

[7] Hubbard, 227.

[8] Warren W. Wiersbe, *Ruth & Esther: Be Committed* (Victor Books, 1993), 49.

[9] Swindoll, 72.

10 Mary E. Byrne (translator) & c. 8th century Irish melody, "Be Thou My Vision" (Chatto and Windus, Ltd., London © Singspiration, Inc., 1968).

CHAPTER NINE

1 Warren W. Wiersbe (adapted), *Ruth & Esther: Be Committed* (Victor Books, 1993), 51.

2 A. Boyd Luter & Barry C. Davis, *God Behind the Seen* (Baker, 1995), 67.

3 Stanley Collins, *Courage and Submission* (Regal Books, 1975), 33.

4 Robert L. Hubbard, *The Book of Ruth* (Eerdmans, 1988), 251.

CHAPTER TEN

1 A. Boyd Luter & Barry C. Davis, *God Behind the Seen* (Baker Books, 1995), 79.

2 Warren W. Wiersbe, *Ruth & Esther: Be Committed* (Victor Books, 1993), 58.

3 Robert J. Morgan, *Nelson's Complete Book of Stories* (Thomas Nelson, 2000), 388.

4 Dr. Arthur Kronhaber in Robert J. Morgan, *Nelson's Complete Book of Stories* (Thomas Nelson, 2000), 388.

5 Ibid., 389.

6 Robert L. Hubbard, *The Book of Ruth* (Eerdmans, 1988), 188.

SCRIPTURE INDEX

OTHER WISDOM COMMENTARIES
BY *Stephen Davey*

Esther

Scandals abound in a drama cast in the ancient Persian Empire. In the midst of political intrigue and betrayal, a beautiful orphan girl suddenly becomes the leading character, as God's providence rescues His people.

At first glance, Esther is the heroine and Mordecai the master manipulator. Take a closer look, however, and you'll discover that God is pulling the strings as His sovereign providence unfolds.

Nehemiah

Nehemiah didn't volunteer for model status, yet his life has been just that. He would rather the spotlight shine on a more deserving follower of God . . . but he's wrong.

As you dust off the memoirs of this ordinary man, you will likely be inspired to serve the faithful God whom Nehemiah follows . . . the One who leads His obedient servant to attempt impossible, extraordinary things for His glory.

Job

In 39 seconds Job's life changed forever. One messenger tripped over another to bring him devastating, heartbreaking news. What Job didn't know was that God had chosen to make him an example of genuine faith in the midst of trying times.

To this day we refer to Job as the example of a suffering saint. Frankly, his life deserves a closer examination . . . and a better imitation from us all.

Titus

Sprinkled throughout the large Metropolis of Crete are congregations of believers in desperate need of godly leadership. But how can Titus, a young pastor, be expected to oversee the development of all these assemblies? The task is grueling, risky, and weighty. Thankfully the Apostle Paul, under Divine inspiration, left Titus with blueprints for the construction – detailed instructions for every question he would face. This letter is the book of Proverbs for the New Testament, and hereas Solomon set the spiritual barometer for every Christian, Paul sets the spiritual barometer for every church.